Discourses
Volume Five
2018

DISCOURSES:
Standing on the
Threshold of Eternity
Volume Five: 2018

Yogacharya David R. Hickenbottom

Editor: Ruth M. Lamb, Ph.D

The Cross and The Lotus Publishing
Camano Island, Washington, USA

Discourses—Volume Five 2018: Standing on the Threshold of Eternity
Copyright ©2023, The Cross and The Lotus Publishing

For permission requests, contact the publisher at:
http://www.crossandlotus.com/contact.html

ISBN: 978-1-957811-05-5 (softcover)
ISBN: 978-1-957811-06-2 (eBook)

All photos courtesy of Carla Hickenbottom Portfolio
unless otherwise attributed (see page 371)

Edited by Ruth Lamb

Book design by Jan Westendorp/Kato Design and Photo (katodesignandphoto.com)

Cover design by Rob Landers, Ruth Lamb, and Jan Westendorp

Printed and bound in the USA

Published by
The Cross and The Lotus Publishing
Camano Island, Washington, USA
Website: www.crossandlotus.com

Contents

OM TAT SAT AUM

Preface

Yogacharya David, Puri, India, 2013.

To stand on the threshold of eternity and sing His song is all there is. And if my voice, my mind, and my heart cannot contain His melody, then He makes me mute and expresses Himself through the great Silence. For, He is the Way, He is the Life, He is all in all: there is nothing but He. These words are stillborn unless He gives them life, and life eternal. For I am His—heart, mind, and soul—He is my Beloved, my infinite Beloved.

This threshold trembles with His power, and it is awe-inspiring. What my Lord is cannot be fit into the small compartment of words—I can only point, so that others are directed toward His Infinite Presence. I am but

His minion, and the "I" is crushed into His holy dust. I am destroyed by Him, yet I live—such is the great paradox of His creation. "Do not be afraid," He whispers. For all is well, all is He—all merge into His Bliss.

None of what I write here can fit into a box, nor a maxim, not even into thought—but must be experienced to be appreciated. For these are His thoughts, and they are mighty, and beyond mind, for they are not my own. He must reveal their truth, their essence, if they are to be truly known—for I stand on the threshold of Eternity.[1]

—YOGACHARYA DAVID

Yogacharya David was inwardly guided to pilgrimage to nature's cathedrals—to immerse himself in vast peace and an immense sense of space. He tells us that it was not his personal will that was at work on this pilgrimage, but the mystical call of the divine—a call to the wilderness. A call that he says he does not understand, but deeply feels to be true. We may ask: What is this call about? Yogacharya David, himself, says that it was not necessarily what his personality wanted for that time. Sri Aurobindo, a great avatar from India, has a perspective that may assist us in our understanding of Yogacharya David's pilgrimage as we journey with him through his 2018 discourses.

In *Essays on the Gita*, Sri Aurobindo summarizes what he feels the divine Teacher Krishna is saying to Arjuna, the great warrior in the Kurukshetra. The Kurukshetra refers to an ancient war that was waged (in India or Persia) when evil and ignorance overcame truth and goodness, rights and fairness, kindness and love. Here in Sri Aurobindo's words, we can hear reverberations of Yogacharya David's words as well, because they both speak of a similar

---

1   From the January 7, 2018 Discourse.

process—uniquely, with Yogacharya David, a 21st-century Western man, seeking the holy vibration of Christ-Krishna consciousness.

"The secret of action," so we might summarize the message of the Gita, the word of its divine Teacher, "is one with the secret of all life and existence. Existence is not merely a machinery of nature, a wheel of law in which the soul is entangled for a moment or for ages; it is a constant manifestation of the Spirit. Life is not for the sake of life alone, but for God, and the living soul of man is an eternal portion of the Godhead. Action is for self-finding, for self-fulfillment, for self-realisation and not only for its own external and apparent fruits of the moment or future . . .

"The supreme, the faultless largest law of action is therefore to find out the truth of your own highest and inmost Existence and live in it and not to follow any outer standard and Dharma. All life and action must be till then an imperfection, a difficulty, a struggle and a problem. It is only by discovering your true self and living according to its truth, its real reality that the problem can finally be solved, the difficulty and struggle overpassed and your doings perfected in the security of the discovered self and spirit turn into a divinely authentic action . . .

"But the consciousness of man is of a double kind and corresponds to the double truth of existence; for there is a truth of the inner reality and a truth of the outer appearance. According as he lives in one or the other, he will be a mind dwelling in human ignorance or a soul founded in divine knowledge."[2]

---

2   (pp. 553–4).

Throughout the discourses, we witness how Yogacharya David's faith grows stronger as his soul-force develops. In his personal sharing, Yogacharya David permits us to view the reality of his inner existence, whereby Nature takes him beyond nature into the realms of Soul and Spirit. The beauty in nature reveals to Yogacharya David the power of Spirit in Nature. This awareness draws him into days of deep superconscious meditation. As he says, the little ego's absorption with the outer world fades in these states, and the genuine truth of humanity's inner reality opens to the grace of the immortal spiritual power. Yogacharya David shares how he loosens the bounded personality and ego desires and enters into a state where divine spiritual will and action are primary. He engages his soul's deepest experiences while touching the supreme.

As we enter the 2018 discourses with Yogacharya David, he greets us with these words:

> The air trembles, the earth is quiet, heaven and nature merge, and the field of infinite power and consciousness waits. This is a perfect moment, and what the Lord chooses or not chooses is held in His almighty hand. For I am wrapped in His ecstasy, and there is nowhere I would rather be. He wants me to be His witness, a reporter from the frontlines of God-consciousness—to speak only the truth of what He gives me—what He reveals to me and makes me experience.[3]

In a series of six volumes of Discourses, Yogacharya David blesses us with his wisdom and his deep understanding of the perilous nature of a climb that can take us to the highest spiritual mountain summits so that we may experience the joy that comes

---

3   January 7, 2018.

from attunement with Spirit, as we too can learn how to reunite soul and spirit so that we can reawaken to who we truly are, and reclaim our life-purpose. Let us join Yogacharya David and climb!

Standing on the Threshold of Eternity is the fifth in a six-volume series of Discourses written by Yogacharya David between 2013 and 2019. The volumes are as follows:

- *Discourses—Volume One: 2013–14: Living a Spiritually Rich Life*

- *Discourses—Volume Two: 2015: Re-Union of Soul and Spirit*

- *Discourses—Volume Three: 2016: A True New Birth*

- *Discourses—Volume Four: 2017: Gateway to the Infinite*

- *Discourses—Volume Five: 2018: Standing on the Threshold of Eternity*

- *Discourses—Volume Six: 2019: Writing in the Book of Life*

Regarding the use of images in this publication: Yogacharya David put great care, creativity, time, and intention into selecting images to complement his writings in each and every posting. When preparing his Discourses for publication, we found that certain images from unknown sources or those which were found to be under copyright could not be included. Every effort has been made to feature replacement images as close as possible to Yogacharya David's original selections. In a few instances where no similar substitute was available, a picture of Yogacharya David or a beloved saint has been offered instead.[4] Substitute images are designated in the caption by a double asterisk **. For example:

---

4   Yogacharya David's original discourses can be found at **www.crossandlotus.com**

Image: Yogacharya David at Anandashram, 2005.** Image attribution is in the Reference section of the book.

OM TAT SAT AUM

Introduction

Yogacharya David, Haridwar, India, 2005.

Dear Aspirant,
    Whenever you begin a journey, you usually start with a destination in mind, a means of conveyance, and a map or landmarks to indicate that you are on the right path. Those of us following this path have God (Self) Realization as our Goal of goals. Our means of conveyance are God-remembrance, such as chanting God's Name, deepened meditation through Kriya Yoga, universal love and service, loving God, and discernment of Truth.

These writings often come in the early morning: a time when the day is quiet and fresh, an open page upon which to write. These thought-expressions come from an unfathomable Source, welling up from the quiet of the all-pervading Spirit. Reading these words has the power to lead you to the same Source from which they have flowed from within me.

The inspiration that fuels these writings comes to me with great power and clarity; however, mere words are incapable of holding all that is given. It is through inner attunement that the power in the words will lift you into the same Spirit that I experience in Super-consciousness, an uplifting power that is a passageway into realms divine.

Human words and thoughts are imperfect; it is only in pure Spirit that perfection is to be truly found. It is the purpose of these writings that we should rise together in the universal Spirit of God. Come, let us soar together and find truth and beauty unencumbered.

These discourses can act as markers upon your spiritual journey to make for safe and rapid progress. Unlike a scattered "hunt and peck" approach, chosen by many taking them on "wild goose chases" only to become thoroughly lost, you will receive teachings of the purest quality that speed you on the most direct path to realization. Obstacles arise, which create challenges for your journey—you can find inspiration here to help you meet those challenges.

These writings contain notes from pilgrimages and journeys that also (reader alert here!) have lessons upon the path embedded in them.[5]

With deepest love and blessings on your journey,
YOGACHARYA DAVID

---

5   This Introduction comes from Yogacharya David's 2013–14 Discourses, Volume One: *Living a Spiritually Rich Life.*

DISCOURSES

January 4

NEW CREATIONS

Nurturing the Light.**

During this New Year's Eve talk, I spoke about everyone having a theme for this coming year by creating a word or phrase that best articulates your primary intention for the year. When I was contemplating last year's theme, *Pilgrimage* came clearly into focus for both Carla and me—perhaps this is no great surprise to you, my faithful readers of these discourses. Seven months, and many thousands of miles around North America, revealed the many spiritual treasures found in this great land: nature's cathedrals, magnificent basilicas, synagogues, and humble wood-clad churches, all radiating their unique and uplifting vibrations. When these holy sites come to mind now, I feel them still resonating within, a blessing endowed by nature, saints, and sincere devotees of God who have imbued these places with a hallowed beneficence for all—especially for those who are spiritually attuned.

Coming to this year, it is now a perfectly new palette upon which to create. What does God wish for the coming year? This is the question that is with me now. 2016 and 2017 were about creating perfect health, and 2015 was about endings and transitions—with the specter of death constantly near me. For this coming year, I know the general feeling, this intuitive sense is perhaps best expressed as: new creations. Creating Mother Hamilton's books is definitely on the program for new creations. I will continue to make progress with these books, in joyful cooperation with those devotees who are working hard on making Mother's transcripts available in book form.

Other creations are coming forward as well: The Cross and The Lotus website improvements,[6] materials for our children with spiritual themes, stories, artwork, and support for Centers and aspirants to make rapid success in Self-realization, as well as some percolating thoughts about home design. All creation begins with an idea on a causal level: everything starts with a conception. Not all ideas achieve physical manifestation—some fulfill themselves as an idea only. And some concepts are seeds for the future—they will not see manifestation immediately but continue to hold great power for their eventual result.

For many years, Mother Hamilton spoke of her intention to author books; however, this did not materialize during her lifetime. Nevertheless, through her weekly talks, Mother was very busy producing the materials that we can now use for that purpose. Her idea-intention of writing books, expressed so many years ago, will find fruition by what is being done now—this is

---

6   www.crossandlotus.com

the power of God's will, expressed through Mother as a causal creation, and using us—her willing instruments—to bring it to completion.

When you have the impulse to create, seek out first the will of God in the matter. This attuning to Spirit avoids false starts, wasted energy, and wrong directions. With clarity of intention, bring the idea into clear view. Some concepts come whole and complete, all in a flash. Many ideas come in seedling form, needing encouragement and attunement to bring out the details. For this work, a calm mind with a pure intention—not selfish or doubting—is the best encouraging soil for seed-creations. Then fertilize the seed-ideas with vibrant energy, activating your enthusiasm and positive vision. With pure intention, from the highest light, and having clarity of purpose and positive energy, take vigorous and active steps toward fulfilling your goal. Attune your mind to the fact that this is God's work, even if it is a material goal such as manifesting prosperity (for all life comes from God). From the very beginning, through the middle parts, and all the way to its completion, God supplies all that you require to have the causal idea, the positive energy, and all you need for the accomplishment of your intention.

By taking these steps with active attunement to the infinite supply, you have the needed strength and courage when obstacles present themselves. There are some who see obstacles as "signs" that they should not continue to the completion of their intentions. But, honestly, what greatness of purpose has not been met with opposition from every side? If doubt assails you, refer to your first step of knowing that this is God's will. When you have thoroughly focused your intention in the first place, then it will serve you as a touchstone to God's pure intention—feel God's strength and purity of purpose. Open yourself to the unlimited resources of God and feel that abundance is flowing to you through creative ideas, the right help from others, new energy infusion, and material resources—all flowing to you, through you, and out to the world from you. You are His instrument, and God delights in making you His co-creator

It is exciting to have a pristine canvas upon which to create as we enter the new year. Know that being made in the likeness and image of God, you too are a joyful creator. Make this year the greatest yet for being His instrument in manifesting His Light, His joy, and His positive creations—all done for the highest good of all.

January 7

STANDING ON THE THRESHOLD OF ETERNITY

The San Damiano crucifix, which inspired St. Francis to "rebuild
My church" and follow the Way of the Cross and the Christ.

The air trembles, the earth is quiet, heaven and nature
merge, and the field of infinite power and consciousness waits. This is a perfect moment, and what the Lord
chooses or not chooses is held in His almighty hand. For I am
wrapped in His ecstasy, and there is nowhere I would rather be.
He wants me to be His witness, a reporter from the frontlines

of God-consciousness—to speak only the truth of what He gives me—what He reveals to me and makes me experience.[7]

I had thought to write about doing His work in the coming year—day by day, stone by stone. Then, I found myself standing on the threshold of Eternity; He gave me the above experience and He made me write it out. And this is His way, at least it is with me. He does not care to consult me in His work, rather He likes me to get out of His way and let Him do it. And whether I look the fool or express His greatest truths is not up to me—for it is only He, only He.

To stand on the threshold of eternity and sing His song is all there is. And if my voice, my mind, and my heart cannot contain His melody, then He makes me mute and expresses Himself through the great Silence. For, He is the Way, He is the Life, He is all in all; there is nothing but He. These words are stillborn unless He gives them life, and life eternal. For I am His—heart, mind, and soul—He is my Beloved, my infinite Beloved. Oh, how He rants, and makes me His sacrifice.

This threshold trembles with His power, and it is awe-inspiring. What my Lord is cannot be fit into the small compartment of words—I can only point, so that others are directed toward His Infinite Presence. I am but His minion, and the "I" is crushed into His holy dust. I am destroyed by Him, yet I live—such is the great paradox of His creation. "Do not be afraid," He whispers. For all is well, all is He; all is a sacred sacrifice for His sacred feast, for He consumes what He creates, and all becomes He—all merge into His Bliss.

None of what I write here can fit into a box, nor a maxim, not even into thought—but must be experienced to be appreciated. For these are His thoughts, and they are mighty and beyond

---

7   Editor's Note: In the interest of copyright rules, we have removed the short quote Yogacharya David placed at the beginning of this discourse. It was a quote from a Donovan song from the St. Francis film, *Brother Sun, Sister Moon.*

mind, for they are not my own. He must reveal their truth, their essence, if they are to be truly known—for I stand on the threshold of Eternity.

January 13

A LUCKY DAY

Happy Birthday, Carla, 2004.

C arla was born on a January day, the 13th—today is her birthday. In celebration of that birth, I want to highlight just some of her outstanding characteristics. First and foremost is her courage in facing obstacles to growth and realization. When she first came to Service, she and I met to discuss the path and answer her questions. Not long after these initial meetings, she demonstrated a keen desire to work on those things that held her back.

One of the first things that was noteworthy was while listening to a talk of Mother's or mine. Carla, later in the week, told me how she had taken a theme from that talk and had been working on it all week. This impressed me greatly. She took something in the talk that stood out to her—meditation, letting her inner Light shine, being on the battlefield of sadhana—and that became her focus as she sought to put it to work in her life.

One of those topics proved to be a watershed moment—it was an in-depth work on prosperity. For years Carla had her own business, then, since moving to the Seattle area, she had worked at several jobs, but did not prosper. In her focused way, we discussed the obstacles to receiving prosperity. There were many levels to it, but through her inner work, doors opened, and within a relatively short time, she was in the adjoining office to, and the personal assistant of, the third-richest man in the world, making the most money she ever had in her life.

The first time Carla came to a Service, she was brought by Peter. Carla heard a tape recording of Mother speaking and knew, for the first time in her life, that this was the truth she had been seeking all these many years. Spiritual life and practice are not easy things, but no matter the ups and downs, the challenges both within and without, Carla has never wavered, never avoided doing her work to tread the path of God-realization. As one of her professors told her, "You are not the first one done, but you keep going until you are." This kind of determination has been a hallmark of Carla's spiritual life and service.

Before and after we married, Carla has been serving this Work we do for Mother and Master. Some things have come at her that would have been a challenge for anyone, but she always focuses on doing her own spiritual work throughout. Many have expressed their gratitude and love for her and the work she does, and this is an opportunity for me to do the same.

Happy Birthday Carla. We are so pleased that you were born on—what for me is— a lucky day, Friday the 13th.

Ever in God and Gurus' blessings.

January 14

CELEBRATING MASTER

Master and Sri Yukteswarji on the
balcony of Serampore Ashram, India, 1936.

When I first met Mother in 1974, I had not heard of the *Autobiography of a Yogi*, or Paramhansa Yogananda. My introduction to Master came from Mother—from her stories, eventually through reading his books, listening to records (yes, LP records) of him singing and talking; then I took a pilgrimage to Mt. Washington, Lake Shrine, and Encinitas. And what a journey it has been to know Master through Mother's experiences, his writings, and his connection to the places where he lived!

I remember Larry and I climbing the stairs to Sri Yukteswarji's Serampore Ashram in India. The steps were worn with use, and I thought—Sri Yukteswar and Master walked up these same steps so many times—I felt so privileged to follow in their footsteps. Then, standing on the same landing where a picture had been taken with Sri Yukteswar standing, and Master sitting, during Yoganandaji's return to India in 1935—it was thrilling. It may be hard for some to understand how meaningful these experiences are, such as meditating in Master's attic meditation room at 4 Gurpar Road in Calcutta, where Master had the vision of the Divine Mother and where Babaji came to see him before his coming to America—what joy there is in this feeling of connection.

Of course, it is not just in physical locations where a realized master resided that he may be experienced. When souls become realized, more than ever, their consciousness may be known wherever a keen desire and love attracts them. When I was at Cloud Mountain, Mother and Master gave me their darshan. In one of those darshans, it was notable that their joy was bubbling over as a deep vibration. That joy repeatedly rose up from some unfathomable source deep inside them—one would start, and the other would respond, and back and forth it went—waves of joy. It was waves of blissful joy after blissful joy that had no limits. Words simply do not do justice; however, the blessings continue with me even now when remembering that evening and will stay with me all the days of my life.

We celebrated Master's birthday on January the fifth, but due to getting medical procedures done at that time, I did not write about it on that day. But I did want to write something about Master's birthday, to say that if not for him, there would be no Mother; without Mother, I do not even want to think of what my life would have been. The living Presence of these masters is the greatest of blessings to all whose minds are attuned to them. As

Lahiri Mahasaya said, to think of Babaji with reverence releases a blessing to you; and so it is with all the great Ones.

It is the power of our thought and devotion that brings God and the masters to us, that gives us an experience with them. Deepened thought and devotion act as a magnet and make them real. There are those who write fanciful tales, and some who mistake or overstate their spiritual experiences, but that should not make us doubt that we may have actual and direct experience with God or any of His saints and realized masters. To think of Master with total devotion will draw him near, and will make you know that his grace and blessings are flowing to you; they will change you and draw you closer to God in body, mind, and soul. Master came to make you know that you may realize God—it is for this reason only that he was born. You can honor him most by going to work, and even as he did, make Self-realization your priority—first, middle, and last.

May Master ever bless you and his grace lift you constantly higher into the supreme divine consciousness of his infinite Beloved.

January 18

PAINFUL YEARNING

Jesus in tremendous distress
in the Garden of Gethsemane,
painting by Carl Bloch, 1873.

A devotee's consciousness reaches out to me, and instantly, I feel his or her distress as my own—it is a painful yearning for God—a desolation, deep and wide. I am put in touch with my many years of such yearning for God and realization. As Mother wrote to Papa so plaintively while in her own despair: "How long, Oh Lord, how long?"

"Oh Lord, why do You wait even a moment when such a cry comes to You from sincere devotees?" And You answer, "Do you not realize that when my son Jesus said you cannot pour new wine into an old wineskin, he was speaking of this very thing?" For this is the truth—the old wineskin of limited human consciousness, and the new wine of Christ Cconsciousness, cannot merge until powerful changes come about that make Divine Consciousness possible in the individual devotee.

The very nerves of the body must be strengthened, or they would be burned out in an instant upon contact with these high-frequency energies. However, through repeated exposure to uplifting experiences, the body system gradually changes, making it a divinely fit instrument. The rising, expanding energy meets the knot points in the spine and brain—a struggle ensues as physical and psychological obstacles keep the new transforming energy from flowing easily and smoothly. Emotional and psychological kinks must be worked out—these kinks are interlocked with physical blockages—the process of sadhana exposes all past emotional obstructions and false, limiting beliefs. Meeting and moving through these mental sticking-points gradually purify the practitioner, for Truth cannot reveal itself when selfishness, greed, fear, and anger loom large. The cup of consciousness must be emptied of all personal attachments—there can be no exceptions.

Through deepened meditation and upliftment, a new body in Christ is generated and brought fully into being. The total yearning of heart, mind, and soul is part of this tremendous cleansing and transformation. Detaching from this world is essential to moving forward on the spiritual path, but this is only part of the story. Letting go of those things that identify you with this body and the world is a must, along with a yearning heart that is full of devotion to God. The first is jnana, discrimination: cutting out whatever is not of transcendent-God. Bhakti, then, is the positive love-thought that draws us to God, and God to us: the wine of Spirit that fills the waiting cup. The yearning pain in the heart sets up a magnetism to which God must respond. Instead of trying to empty the mind of self only, which can have negative consequences, the positive thought of God fills the mind with light, love, and devotion—making for a healthy psychological outlook.

Even though yearning for God can be tremendously painful as your heart breaks in its desire for the universal vision, your increasing devotion now becomes a more powerful force in the psyche and supersedes the attachment to the senses. Bliss, upliftment, joy, loving service, and a positive desire for the Divine fill you, and propel you, to the ultimate Goal of goals. Love and discrimination work together, along with selfless service to others and a growing drive to enter into the highest states of meditative-union that becomes all-consuming.

So, I feel the painful yearning of the devotee who is at such a great distance away—and it is my pain as well. God has given me this life where I experience the various moods and states of mind of aspirants—these moods are all deeply familiar to me. And now, pain is also bliss, for there is no fear—I know this is what it takes to crack open the seedling-heart that reveals the Soul to the soul. Even in the excruciating pain, I know this absolutely, and therefore, it is also endless joy—for it is the harbinger of so much goodness and light to come. Victory to God—Victory to the Light—may unbounded love, and keen discrimination, ever guide the way for devotees, so that all may find the flawless way to the one infinite Lord.

January 20

THE GREAT SWAMI VIVEKANANDA

Swami Vivekananda, Jaipur, India, c. 1885–1895.

On January 20th, 1929, Swami Yogananda attended a banquet in New York honoring the birth of the remarkable Swami Vivekananda. This brought to my mind the great God-man who preceded Master's coming to America by 27 years. Swami Vivekananda was recognized as a prodigious soul by his own guru, Ramakrishna Paramhansa when he was yet a student at the age of 19. Ramakrishna later told some devotees that in one of his visions, he had traveled to the Causal Realm where he met an amazing Being. He, Ramakrishna, asked that Being if he would incarnate here on earth and help him with his mission. Years later when Vivekananda, then known by his birth name Narendranath, walked through his door, Ramakrishna recognized Vivekananda as the great soul he had earlier called to earth.

Vivekananda was born to a well-to-do family, but his father died when he was in college. It fell to the young man to provide for his mother and eight siblings. Even in this time of stress, he came to see his master, but it was far from a smooth journey. Vivekananda had a brilliant mind and was very independent. At first, he doubted Ramakrishna's state of realization, then he went through a time of intellectual doubt and atheism. When other devotees were distressed by Vivekananda's outspoken views, including his doubts, Ramakrishna would comfort them by saying that Vivekananda would never succumb to the temptations of "women and gold," that he was one of a rare breed who would never be ensnared by ignorance.

By the time his master passed, Vivekananda was keen to become a monk. After some time living with his brother disciples, he struck out on his own and walked the circumference of India. As he traveled south, he had deep questions in his mind: How was he to serve humanity? What was his mission? At the very south point of India, on a rock where the Bay of Bengal, the Indian Ocean, and the Arabian Sea meet, he determined to meditate until he had the answer. Without food or water, he sat for days. Suddenly, he had a magnificent vision of his guru and the history of India—he knew what he was here to do.

From there, he traveled northward up the east coast; whereas before he had been fairly incognito, now masses of people responded to him. He felt he was to go to America, to the first *Parliament of the World's Religions,* which was to open on September 11, 1893. He came without knowing about, or having the kind of recommendations that were required to be a speaker at the Parliament; nevertheless, through an amazing series of events, he was invited to be a speaker. At the end of the first day, he was to give a talk to over seven thousand participants. Several of the speakers before had been rather dull, the audience subdued. The end of a long day is an unenviable time to give a talk. Swamiji was nervous. He prayed before a statue of Saraswati, the goddess of learning; he felt his master with him. He started his speech, "Sisters and brothers of America!" For two minutes after he finished, there was a thunderous standing ovation!

From there, speaking engagements were scheduled. A couple of incidents stand out in my memory of the master. One happened when Vivekananda was giving a talk at a church in a small community. A mentally deranged man entered the church and fired a gun at Swamiji. Those in the pews dove for cover as the bullets flew. Meanwhile, Vivekananda stood up front, facing the man without moving. He calmly gazed at the man firing his gun until the gunman ran out of bullets!

Another interaction involved a famous man of the times. John D. Rockefeller was one of the richest men in the world. Friends told him he should meet the "extraordinary Indian monk." Rockefeller was strong-willed, independent, and had no intention of doing so. But one day, he somehow decided to go see this man of God from India. He came to the house where Swamiji was staying. The butler asked Rockefeller to wait, but he charged past the butler and entered the study where Swamiji was writing. Rockefeller waited. After some time, Swamiji without raising his eyes, started telling Rockefeller about his life: things that even his closest friends did not know. Then Swamiji told the multi-millionaire that the money he had was not his own. God had given him these resources to help others—the poor, and the distressed—Swamiji finished by saying that Rockefeller should spend his money for the benefit of society.

Rockefeller left as abruptly as he had come—he was not used to people speaking to him that way! About a week later, he returned to the house and entered the study where, once again,

Swamiji was busy writing. Rockefeller put a newspaper on the table that had headlines about a large amount of money he had donated to a public institution and said, "There you are. You must be satisfied now. You can also thank me for this." Swamiji, who did not lift his eyes, picked up the paper and read. Then he said, "Why should I thank you? Rather, you should thank me for providing the suggestion." Later, this gift of money was followed by other large donations by the millionaire and eventually led to the establishment of the Rockefeller Foundation in 1913.

Each incident of a person's life is like a puzzle piece that, when put together, builds a picture of the whole person—however, we will never have all the pieces to any one person, much less that of such a highly God-realized Soul as Swami Vivekananda. The close of Swamiji's life for this incarnation came on the 4th of July, 1902. He started the day by meditating for three hours, then he taught a class on the philosophy of yoga to young students, and later, he led a discussion for the planning of a Vedic College. When he went to his room, he asked not to be disturbed. Swami Vivekananda left the body at 9:20 that night while meditating. Doctors said the cause of death was a burst blood vessel in his brain—devotees said the blood vessel burst when the master pierced his crown chakra, the brahmarandhra, while entering Mahasamadhi. He was 39 years old. His guru had said many years before that once his disciple tasted the full freedom of God, he would in that moment leave the body.

January 24

REALIZATION IS RELIGION

Dove of Peace.

Religion takes on many forms all around this world, sometimes with seemingly contradictory ideas. The contradictions usually boil down to, "I am right and all others are wrong." However, a true analysis of all the great religions shows that each one was based on a series of revelations by a few master-souls; these revelations are then instituted into formalities, ceremonies, and articles of belief. These forms, originally based on revelations, are then objectively called religion. As Mother Hamilton said: "God made man, and man made religion."

However, the symbols in these revelations are meant to be roadmaps for aspirants, helping to guide them to achieve their own direct perception of Truth. In the normal course of history, this goal is soon forgotten or disbelieved by religionists. Institutions hold up the revelations and say, "Worship these with faith." The fact that these original revelations are meant to lead to individual revelations of the Heavenly Father and Divine Mother is now seen as heresy. Those striving for a fresh knowledge of God are many times convicted of crimes by such institutions. The truth is stood on its head—the real goal is forgotten, and even seen as evil. Such is the repeated story of religion all around the globe, and down through time.

Although prophets, men and women of God, come periodically to remind us of the supreme truth, their message quickly falls into obscurity. However, there has never been a time when ultimate truth did not exist, only that it became lost to the majority. That need never be the case—ever again. Collectively, we can stand up and proclaim the Truth of truths: realization is religion; there is no religion without realization; and, religion loses its most profound meaning when it fails to raise others up to the heights of realization. With a renewed synergistic relationship between realization and religion, the tremendous potential of humanity is unleashed.

To make this truth a living reality, there must be those who are willing to follow the way of saints and spiritual masters—to strive for realization, and to revitalize the lifeblood of the living Spirit for aspiring souls. New hope for new times—through renunciation of attachment to this world, and through a complete surrender to the supreme Being, the Divine can shine through its perfected beings and raise this world to greater heights.

The angel Gabriel is sounding his trumpet, calling all to the revelatory altar of the one true living God—this "Call" reverberates across space, and opens wide the way for truth. Yes, there will be false prophets along the way; that is inevitable. However, there will also be true God-men and God-women who will bless this earth and all humankind, who will reveal the truth and awaken other men and women across the globe, thereby bringing this world into higher states of illumination. There is no limit to this transformation. It all starts with those who are responsive to the call of truth and with those who have the courage to seek it out. They will know deep within themselves that attaining a direct perception of God is their real purpose in life: that all religions are, in reality, here to guide and support those striving for the realization of their eternal being and existence.

January 28

MOTHER HAMILTON'S LAUGH

Mother Hamilton, 1981.

On Wednesday January 31st, we mark the anniversary of Mother's Mahasamadhi. While it is certainly a solemn occasion to observe the time of Mother consciously leaving the body, and we certainly recognize the tremendous contribution Mother has made to our lives, what stands out for me, in this moment, is Mother's sense of humor and fun—Mother's laugh. The streets of Mother's joy and wisdom often met at the intersection of laughter—using humor in her work as God's minister and purely in comical appreciation of the general human condition.

On one occasion Mother said:

> As many of you who see more of me perhaps than others do, you know that I have a tremendous sense of humor, and that I do a lot of wisecracking, and sometimes it seems to get out of control. This evening I was reading briefly out of a book called *The Master Said,* which told about incidents in my own guru's life. He said that when he was a boy, he used to laugh a lot, and that the saints he went to see just loved his laughter. I was thinking the other day that when I get up to the pearly gates, because I've laughed and joked so much and sometimes taken God along with me, that I might be in a little trouble with Him. Either He is going to say, "Well, here is this terrible person that didn't hang her head in shame and think of all the sins she has committed and whatnot," or He's going to say, "Well, here comes this individual who doesn't think she has to wear sackcloth and ashes all the time and starve the body and whatnot," and maybe He'll just welcome me into His arms. So, this story reminded me of that. Master told about his going to all these saints and how they loved his laughter, but one saint said to him, "You know, I understand your laughter. But sometimes when you laugh like that so wholeheartedly, you annoy the other devotees." And Master said to him, "But it is God who laughs." And the saint said, "Yes, that is true. You may laugh if you wish." (Chuckles) So, I take that.[8]

Mother, Master, and Papa all had a tremendous sense of fun—they could laugh at themselves as well as the recurring

---

8   www.crossandlotus.com for Mother Hamilton's quotes.

absurdities of life. Sri Yukteswarji also had a wonderful, some-times wry, sense of humor. After Sri Yukteswar was recovering from a serious illness, Master wrote: When I ventured a few words of sympathy over his emaciated figure, my guru said gaily: "It has its good points; I am able now to get into some small *ganjis* (undershirts) that I haven't worn in years!"

Listening to Master's jovial laugh, I remembered the words of St. Francis de Sales: "A saint that is sad is a sad saint!"

From a talk Mother gave, it shows her way of using humor to make a salient point with everyday imagery:

> But, you know, there are a lot of people who just love to borrow trouble, so I brought along a little recipe for misery. (Laughter.) I thought I'd like to share it with you. If you'd like to take it down—if you have paper and pen-cil . . . (Laughter.) It calls for one cup of guilt, one cup of dwelling on the past, one-half cup of plain "poor me," a pinch of sarcasm, one tablespoon of criticism, one-fourth cup of blaming others. Blend and let it set until the ego rises to double its size. (Tremendous laughter.) Divide it in equal portions and bake in a hot oven of judgment. (Laughter.) I think that's beautiful.

As we know, Jesus was a master storyteller who made his points while giving memorable images to his listeners. Mother could also use funny stories to a wonderful, even to a devastating, effect as she did in telling this story:

> When you have final God realization, you see, one thing is like another to you. You cannot see any differ-ence because there is God equally present everywhere. But our egos are so great, and we think that if we have accomplished a little something, that it is we who have

done it. In truth, we have done nothing. It is God who has done all of it.

There was a very capable man, one day, who was a good businessman. He had talked to a great number of people, and his talk had been extremely successful. He was lauded as a wonderful orator, and everybody said what a wonderful speech he had given. The praise that was given to him was beyond description.

The next morning, he got up and he dressed. He was before the mirror shaving and combing his hair, when he really looked in the mirror. He said to his wife, "How many great men do you really think there are in the world?"

His wife looked at him, and she said, "Well, I don't know, but I can tell you one thing. There is one less than you think." I think that is a wonderful, wonderful story.

While the path can be tough, keeping a sense of humor about our human condition helps ease us along the way; it makes us not take ourselves too seriously, and it can make a point to the other person in a way that may be of help—and do it with a laugh. We do not need to be the saint who goes around being sad, thinking that by doing so we are pleasing God—for that, indeed, would make us a sad saint.

With love in our hearts, we strive to be more like our dear Mother, delightful Master, and joyous Papa—we can clap our hands and ask, "What's the fun?"

January 30

MY BELOVED PAPA: IN HONOR OF MOTHER

Mother Hamilton sitting at the feet of Papa
at Anandashram Bhajan Hall, 1957–58.

January 31 is Mother's Mahasamadhi date, and we mark the day by celebrating Mother's life as one of the greatest God-women this world has seen. When Master incarnated, he brought some tremendous souls with him—among those greats were Sister Gyanamata (Edith Bissett), and of course Mother Hamilton. Both lived in Seattle and became friends as sister-disciples of Master Paramhansa Yogananda. Sister moved down to live with Master, Mother remained in Seattle. In subsequent years, Master made Mother the Center Leader of Seattle, ordained her a minister, and then Master gave Mother the distinction of being the only woman with the title of Yogacharya in his worldwide work.

As Reverend Lawrence Koler and Cate, and Reverend Jill were all at Anandashram during the preparation of a booklet in celebration of this date, we focused on the writings of Mother to Swami Ramdas—the booklet is entitled *My Beloved Papa, Swami Ramdas*.[9] These very important letters show the progress of Mother's journey to God-realization.

Mother's teachings are unique, in that the experiences that God put her through are her teachings. When Mother completed a spiritual experience, God would guide Mother to a biblical passage and the connection between her experience and the biblical passage would be revealed to her. Such revelations may seem ephemeral or even haphazard to someone only just hearing about this—however, such realizations affect every part of a person: body, mind, and soul. The knowledge gained in this way does not come as an idea only, but as an entire experience that changes the aspirant down to the cellular level of body and being. These letters from Mother to Papa trace the impact he had on Mother from their first meeting in Seattle to Mother's return from Anandashram and her "Dark Night of the Soul". May Mother's writings inform and inspire you, and ultimately lift you into the supreme Divine Consciousness.

I have always felt that to truly honor Mother Hamilton, her life, and her teachings, is to follow in her footsteps. I consider Mother the greatest saleswoman in the world, for she would tell us that to follow her would mean that we would enter the *Mystical Crucifixion:* it will be difficult, painful, tear us down—even to the point of death—before lifting us up in God-consciousness. Now, who wants to sign up?

---

9   This booklet entitled *My Beloved Papa, Swami Ramdas* is available at www.crossandlotus.com

Mother is leading us on the most terrific adventure known to humanity. Even though the saying from Star Trek has been made famous—"Space, the final frontier"—I think the true ultimate frontier is inner space through spiritual evolution. Mother is our leader, and those of us who choose are the lucky explorers in humankind's greatest adventure. Thank you, Mother, for leading the way with your courage, faith, loyalty, and purity of purpose—and for your compassion for us all through all the years you taught us while focusing on our spiritual advancement.

Note: There is an interesting astronomical event on Mother's Mahasamadhi Anniversary that is occurring for the first time in 150 years. It is a Super Blood Blue Moon. Super, because it is in a near-orbit to earth; therefore, large and bright—as evidenced yesterday when I saw the moon in the afternoon. It was big and brilliant, even in daylight. It is called a Blood Moon because it will be eclipsed; in the earth's shadow, it will appear dark red. For those on the West Coast, the total eclipse will be shortly after 6 a.m. And it is also a Blue Moon; you know, "Once in a Blue Moon," that is, it is the second full moon in one month. I often feel the effects of the moon's cycles, and the timing of this rare occurrence is interesting. You may want to observe your meditation during this time to mark its effects—and even take a peek outside at this rare astronomical event.

February 4

A Strange Reversal

Moon over red hills of Lake Cahuilla, the morning
after Mother's Mahasamadhi Anniversary.

It has happened over time that my mind has become even more inwardly focused. As a part of this experience, it happens that when I am at even a great distance from dear ones, I feel so very closely connected to them. When on the phone or in person, there are times when a great pressure builds, and my brain soon becomes overheated. There are exceptions to this, but on the whole, this is my state.

I have questioned: Mother: "Why choose me as God's minister?" A role normally filled by one who revels in the world of social circumstances, whereas God has increasingly made me a recluse. This withdrawal has definitely been at His instigation, both by His command and in the way He makes me experience this world.

God's love so powerfully flows through me, but so often, it does so best at a distance. Usually, human relationships feel closest when there is a close physical proximity—but God has given me this strange reversal. Such is the mystery of this life God has given me.

On another note, the uplifting power of Mother's Mahasamadhi Anniversary continues with me. I feel her power and glory resonating within, and in the ether all about me. This reality of knowing God in Mother, and Mother in God, makes the world tremble with holy vibration. In truth, I feel myself to be totally empty—God and Gurus' Presence is all there is. How can I look out on the world and say God is this, and not that, when there is only one: one Spirit, one God, and one supreme Reality, that is all and all in all!

God seems to be in a funny mood as He writes this through me, wandering from subject to subject according to His whim!

There is a story that comes to mind about a disciple of Master's, who went to see Swami Ramdas. When he asked Papa to be his guru, Papa replied to the man that he already had one, Master. But, the man replied, "My guru is dead." Papa replied, "Your guru is not dead—you are."

Resurrect in us O great Ones Your wondrous Presence! Make us live, not as the worldly live, for they are dead to You. Renew us in your Living Waters. Bring us wonder and beauty, joy and love, unceasingly.

The Galilean Master said you cannot serve two masters; you must choose—either serve God or serve the world. You definitely live in this world, and you must render unto Caesar what is Caesar's; however, there should never be a doubt about who your true master is—who is central to your heart, mind, and soul, and who it is that you are truly serving.

February 8

Into the Sonoran Desert

Vulture Peak, Arizona.

God has completed some much-needed work where we had been staying and has now moved us on to BLM (Bureau of Land Management) land, Federal land that allows campers and RVs (Recreational Vehicles) to stay for no fee. These are primitive roads and campsites—campers are expected to take care of the land, and people here are wonderfully responsible.

The previous work regarded changing the vibration of a place where a tragedy had occurred. There are times when we enter a space and just know that something terrible happened there.

This feeling of calamity can be changed by devotees through God-remembrance—chanting God's name, feeling His light and bliss, and experiencing God's all-pervading Presence. Through such remembrance, we can change a negative vibration into a positive one. With this work done, we were free to move on.

We now find ourselves at a location we have been to before, where we have always felt we would like to return. We have entered the vast Sonoran Desert at a beautiful spot with an unlovely name, Vulture Peak, Arizona. Poor vultures get a bad name; they are ungainly looking, but magnificent flyers, known for picking over already dead carcasses. We are in a forest of saguaro cacti; the Sonoran Desert is the only place in the world where they grow naturally. In 25 years, this cactus will shoot up all of two feet from the ground, and through many years, it can eventually gain a sixty-foot height. Birds, cacti, and bushes of many kinds abound—far from empty, this desert is positively teeming with life.

We recently were staying in some beautiful man-icured places, and appreciate what that brings—visual beauty, a controlled environment, and friendly people. However, the rustic beauty of this desert has an openness and a clean vibration where our souls can expand and have room to breathe. It is much to my liking, and this has been our aim. It is a wonderful thought that on these dates, Master was in nearby Phoenix in 1931, teaching a series of classes. Just the thought of Master brings a spiritual blessing with it.

On another positive note, Mother Hamilton continues to clear the way for me to work on her writings. We have a virtual office where devotees work from their own homes, producing important contributions to make Mother's books become a reality. I think Mother left us this work to do as a means of keeping our minds on her and learning how God uniquely expressed Himself through her words. It is an immense project, and it will take some time yet before it is completed. However, it is heartening to see continued progress toward our goal.

Mother really is such a tremendous God-personality. And we have been privileged to have Master's many written works—a tour-de-force that grew from his meditations and affirmations, his poems, prayers, and lessons, his classic *Autobiography of a Yogi*, and his magnum-opus commentaries on the *Bhagavad Gita* and *The Second Coming of Christ*.

Mother's books will blaze the trail on several spiritual themes. One of the most important, and the topic she came to bring to light, is the inner meaning of the Bible. How beautifully her teachings dovetail with Master's Gita and his *Second Coming of Christ*, bringing the truth of original Christianity to all the world.

Scriptures are mysterious, in as much as they originate from the intuitive insights of highly realized souls—often coming directly from their God-consciousness. With divine origins such as these, there are so many ways that the teachings in scripture can apply to an aspirant. From learning the ABCs of a spiritual life: tell the truth, do not murder, show respect for others, all the way to the highest mystical meanings concerning the death of the ego, and the resurrection of God-consciousness. Through Mother's experiences, during her sixteen years in the Mystical Crucifixion, and her attaining ultimate oneness with her infinite Beloved, she was able to reveal the deepest meanings of the Christian scriptures that had laid hidden in obscurity for nearly two thousand years. The world stands on the cusp of awakening to these higher truths. Mother has come as an example, paving the way for a world that yearns for the truth. And, as our great and dear Galilean Master said, "And ye shall know the truth and the truth shall make you free" (John 8:32).

February 11

METRICS FOR REALIZING GOD

Sunset from Vulture Peak: like a halo, dramatic colors surrounded
us all the way around—God painting bold watercolor strokes.

The spiritual principles we have been taught are simple to comprehend, but not always easy to practice. Mother simplified the whole spiritual path down to this: *Keep your mind on God.* You do not need to believe in reincarnation; you do not even need to know who God is—you do not need to worry about so many of the things taught, but you do need to learn to focus your mind.

If you do not need to know God to start this journey, then what does it mean to put your mind on God? It means you focus your mind in a singular fashion, in the highest way you know. You may repeat the name of God without any great knowledge of what God is in the beginning, practice the mantra Hong Sau without knowing the great I AM—in fact, truthfully, you will not fully know God, or who your real Self is, until you have become realized.

This lack of knowledge was my situation when I met Mother. I did not have a cultivated belief in a God, and I definitely did not know who I was in Spirit. But what I did have were some experiences that made me know there was a God, and whatever that was, it helped me in a time of great need. That was my starting point. I had read about reincarnation, and my first thought was, "Of course." But I did not have any real knowledge of it beyond my intuitive affirmation. Much of what Mother taught was new to me, and I was determined that I was not going to be "sold a bill of goods," meaning I wasn't going to go along with something just because someone said it. I was a tough sell. What I did have was a driving need to resolve the spiritual pain I found myself in, and I needed to know the truth.

So, in short, to be a good spiritual scientist, you do not need, nor is it beneficial, to pose as knowing more than you know, pretending to have experienced more than you have experienced, or project to others that you are realized when you are yet walking in darkness. The goal of knowing God does not go to the clever-minded, persons with gifted speech, or the ones who present themselves as leaders of the pack. Those who know God are, above all else, sincere, pure-minded, and of soft heart—they continually focus on attaining the supreme state of realization—they are simple, unpretentious, and dedicated to truth.

As an aspirant, you are humble enough to know what your strengths are, what deficiencies you have, and how well you are focused on attaining the Goal of goals. This humble assessment gives you, what in the field of psychology is called, a baseline. If you do not have an accurate idea of where you are starting, you will have no means of knowing your progress. Humility makes you not be overly hard on yourself, for this lack of self-worth is not the truth, nor does it over-inflate your opinion of your own progress, for this would be based on a lie.

Sri Yukteswarji gave us a metric for knowing God: Do you experience ever-new joy? Swami Satchidananda gave us another: Is your circle of love growing larger every day? For Mother: Do you continuously keep your mind dwelling on God? Master asks: Do you dive deeper into your daily meditations until you get God contact? Lahiri Mahasaya: Do you perceive your true Self at the ajna? Babaji states: It is your humble service to humankind that the Lord finds pleasing above all. And Papa's ideal: Continuously chant Ram Nam. Here are measurements, metrics, for your spiritual path. Read each of these again; make them a challenge; let your practice dive deeper and soar higher—answer the call of your Soul to know God, and be a blessing to this world.

February 14

ASH WEDNESDAY

Ash Wednesday.**

oday is Ash Wednesday, marking about 40 days until Easter—it is a time of repentance. The Ash part comes from a tradition of placing some ashes over the head, or using ash to mark a cross on the forehead, saying the words, "Repent, and believe in the Gospel," or "Remember that you are dust, and to dust you shall return." (Not very cheery, and it would only be true if we were the body.) Interestingly, yogis put ashes on their bodies to help cool them—originally for when having kundalini experiences.

Thinking of repenting, turning back to God, and preparing ourselves for the Mystical Crucifixion, we can reflect on anything that interferes with our communion with God. It is traditional to give up something for the 40 days in the buildup to Easter, and it is a good time to renounce any obstacle. Some people give up sweets, others television; it could be the cell phone and electronics (or limit their usage, such as the insane practice of texting while driving!). Remove whatever comes to mind that interferes with receptivity to God awareness.

I thought that as part of paying homage to this day we could enjoy reading a part of a talk Mother gave on Ash Wednesday:

> As I'm sure all of you know, today is the beginning of the Lenten season. It is Ash Wednesday. So, I call this to your attention in order that you might enter into the spirit of the Lenten season, that you might fast from some of the things which you ordinarily enjoy, both in the sense of food and the things of the senses.
>
> This Lenten season actually depicts the story of each individual soul as that one starts on the higher rungs of the ladder of God-realization. The whole Christian world has come to think of it as a time of deep sorrow, and it is that indeed because what man has to go through in order to become a Godman, or the Christed one—the son of God—is indeed not easy. Every little bit of the price must be paid for the *pearl*, which is the supreme jewel of God-realization. There can be no holding back if you would attain that greatest of all boons, if you would have the petals of your flower of God-realization open wide and spread forth the light which is your True Self. It is a very necessary part of your journey through life at some time or other, if you, as you must do, would realize your oneness with the Divine within yourself. There are many trials, many tests, many tribulations, and in some cases, a great deal of pain, before that sublime moment is reached.

In the early days of the Christians, this custom was started. It is difficult to know exactly when because practically all of the feast days were tied up with some of the Pagan rites that existed long before the birth of Christ, and this one is no exception. Again, it was a case of celebrating the change of the seasons. They had a funeral ceremony, and they had a snowman to represent the death of snow and the beginning of spring. Where there's usually the ordinary amount of food taken, then at that time, gradually, the rules were made to stop eating all things of the flesh, all flesh meats and the products thereof, such as cheese and milk, eggs and butter. We have come a long way from those times, and perhaps it is well that we bring them to remembrance.

May this Lenten Season bring us closer to God, Christ, and Gurus, and may we use this as an opportunity to sharpen our focus on God, surrendering all that we are at the feet of our most Beloved One.

Happy Valentine's Day! It brings to mind something we did in grade school. We made decorated folders that hung off the front of our desks. Everyone in the class created cards for each other to drop into the folders. This is my version of dropping a Valentine's card off in your folder.

Happy Valentine's Day.

February 18

LOOK DEEPER: THERE IS HIS LIGHT

Sunrise, Picacho Peaks, Arizona.

God has been filling my time and life to the full during our desert stay. We are currently at a state park near Tucson, Arizona, a lovely spot surrounded by a forest of saguaros, and views of the Picacho Peaks. Even though there are nice hikes here, God has not let me venture out from this living space.

The way He works in this form is extraordinary, and I am in constant awe at what He does. This recent past has been a battle with astral powers and entities. There was a time during my Mystical Crucifixion when these entities were prevalent. Following Mother's example, I kept my mind on God, determined to have His Light and power first, middle, and last. This last week there have been times when the fight has been fierce, but I have no fear of them or what they can do, for I know that Light is greater than darkness, love eradicates fear, and peace transcends mischief-making and turbulence.

During the evening hours a week ago, I felt a tremendous burning on the back of my neck. There was no outward reason for this—God told me this was a dark astral force at work. It left a red burn mark and several puncture-type wounds that remained for much of the week. The initial pain was terrific, like being branded on the inside; the after-effect was a constant pain that gradually subsided, along with the marks and then healing. God let me know this was all connected with a dear soul who needed some help in their experiences, and it coincided with a tragic event where school children were murdered. It is powerful and wonderful how God works in this way to help resolve difficulties, even from great distances.

Later in the week, a strange astral force stung the back of my hand with pins and barbs—nothing material could be seen to cause this sharp pain. During this same period, I was aware that astral forces were trying to gain entry into my being—all this, and an item that simply disappeared—has made this quite a week. Mother spoke of battling these forces, and her powerful declaration that she would not allow these forces to prevail. With an absolute focus on the Light, there is no doubt about the outcome—God will prevail; it is a matter of striving forward and keeping Him first.

There was a time when Papa said that "recently" strange things had been occurring, and Swamiji said, "Only lately, Papa!" In truth, God's work always keeps things interesting. There is nothing I would rather be doing than His work, to be His instrument. Even if He takes me to places that challenge me to the core, it is only an opportunity for Him to demonstrate His ultimate power and intelligence for overcoming.

Is there any place that God is not? He is everywhere-present. Even in His greatest darkness—look deeper and behold His Light, the first-born of all creation.

February 22

INTEGRITY MAKES THE DIFFERENCE

George Washington, portrait by Rembrandt Peale, 1846.

O n February 22, we celebrate George Washington's Birthday. Washington was the one indispensable man in the American revolution—a revolution that was not just for the citizens of this country, but a revolution that set into motion a Republic built on Democratic principles that would prosper and eventually be duplicated around the world. It was Washington's strength of character, and quiet but strong belief in God, that sustained him as a general, and as the first president. His place in history was secured when he voluntarily stepped down from power without choosing his successor—a first in history. I have borrowed a quote from the Ananda website concerning Master's comments on this great soul.

Yogananda visited Washington's tomb and offered flowers on this day in history, 1927.

Yogananda visited Mount Vernon with his students and gave a talk. A photograph was taken, showing him leaving a wreath at Washington's grave. His words to the audience included the following:

> As Washington performed his duty, he never forgot the Giver of all gifts. That is what inspired me in his life. In India, he always inspired me with this thought. His love for Truth was greater than love of party politics. I believe that though patriotism is necessary, it should not exclude Spiritual Truth because patriotism which excludes international well-being is built on loose stones. But patriotism which is firmly built on the everlasting source of Truth, that patriotism which loves Truth and Truth Alone, that nation is based on such patriotism as Washington possessed and the great good that he did to the world and

to America is ever awake with us. He is ever living in the minds of the world, and we must always be inspired by his example for he inspired not only thousands, hundreds of thousands, but millions.[10]

We also reflect on one of the great personalities of these past one hundred years, as Billy Graham passed away at the age of 99. He was a powerful orator; he dedicated his life to issuing out the call to accept Jesus Christ as one's personal Lord and Savior. He was noted for his ethical life, at a time when many famous preachers have fallen into disrepute. He was the most widely known preacher of his day, and he inspired many to change their lives. Here is an excerpt I found insightful, about this dedicated servant of Jesus, from a tribute that Larry sent to me that was written by Cal Thomas, a columnist.

In my long career in journalism, I have met many famous people, but none of them impressed me as much as William Franklin "Billy" Graham. The reason had less to do with his fame and movie star looks; it was his humility that was so attractive, so refreshing, so like the One he faithfully served.

My conversations with him quickly turned to me. He wanted to know about my family, how I was doing. Politicians do this, too, but often it is a manipulative technique. With Graham, it was real. It is why so many loved him, including those who do not share his faith.

Graham desegregated his meetings long before it became "fashionable." Especially in the South this was a dangerous thing to do in the 1950s. He once told me of a conversation he had with Dr. Martin Luther King, Jr. in which he quoted King as saying to him about desegregation and civil rights, "You take the stadiums and I'll take the streets."

In a 1979 interview I conducted with him for a book called *Public Persons and Private Lives: Intimate Interviews*, Graham told me that the accolades he had received shocked him because he did not feel worthy to preach. In others, this might seem like false humility, but not with Graham. I had observed him long enough to know that the light grace of humility rested easily on him.

Graham said he "felt everything (the Apostle) Paul felt"—inadequate, sinful and weak in the flesh. And then he said, "I've been asked 'How do you feel when you stand up to preach?' Usually, I feel totally inadequate and wish that the floor would open up and let me drop through. There are many times when I stand up that I almost feel like running from the stadium. I feel like I have nothing to give these people . . . And then I remember that it's the power of the Word. It's not me."

"I'd be delighted to go today," he told me. "I look forward to death. In a way, I suppose it's because I've studied a great deal in the Scriptures concerning Heaven. I believe it's going to be something beyond anything that we could imagine. Death is going to be a wonderful experience. I hope they don't dope me up. I want to experience death, because I think even the suffering is a part of life and that in suffering, we gain spiritual strength."

And, I ask, what will you say to the Christ whom you have served most of your life when you see Him?

"I know I'm going to fall down before him and say, 'Lord forgive me,' I think that's what I'll say."[11]

---

11   https://www.savannahnow.com/story/opinion/columns/2018/02/24/cal-thomas-billy-graham-i/13608487007/

February 25

LIBERATING SURRENDER

Jesus and Peter on the Water, painting by Gustave Brion, 1863.**
Peter overcomes fear, and looks to his master in complete faith and
surrender in order to rise above the tumultuous waves of doubt.

Surrender is key to finding God-realization—we hear the
words, receive the teachings, yet life hits us where it hurts
and we find ourselves caught in the web of conflicting reactions—love and hate, attraction and repulsion, like and dislike,
plans made and plans frustrated. We think we are prepared to
surrender, but then we say, "Oh no, not that!"

On top of how life seems to go after the very things we want
to protect, there is also the complication of knowing exactly
what surrender means. In modern vocabulary, surrender oftentimes means giving in, throwing in the towel, and giving up in

defeat. When we look at the lives of great spiritual masters and saints, we see that this is obviously not what is meant, for these unstoppable personalities fight remarkable battles on the human front—persevering when the world stands against them, giving their lives in ceaseless activity, and in some instances, literally. There is no hint of becoming flaccid when it comes to standing up for truth, virtue, and God.

This surrender is not giving in to the world, the body, or desire nature; rather, it is total abandonment to God's will. Anyone who has lived much of a life can look back and see many "lifetimes" within this one life—various stages where life takes radical changes and turns us in completely new directions from the way we had been going. This can be particularly true of one who has surrendered to the will of God. While there is no template that God-realized souls follow, many times each one found their lives following a very different course from their assumed natural trajectory. Lahiri Mahasaya met Babaji, and the great master was directed back into family life and career when all he wanted to do was to stay with his beloved guru. Papa Ramdas was married, had a young daughter, and his direction from God took him into a wandering sannyasa life, one without any outer support but God alone. Both of these great masters had to completely surrender all their ideas of what they thought they wanted, or should do, to the will of God's direction.

I look back over my life, and I see how many times that, if I had listened better and surrendered completely at the time, how much suffering and misdirection I would have saved. On the other hand, I also look at when, beyond everything I wanted, or thought I should do, I surrendered heart, mind, and soul to God and Gurus, and how I, and others, ultimately benefited. There have been times when what God directed was not met with approval by those around me, and these times have been the most difficult for me. Other points of surrender are when my life took turns that were surprising and unwanted, and I **did not** surrender to illness, lack of prosperity, frustrated attempts to meet goals, or the myriad of other problems life presented. But I did surrender to the fact that it was God who was orchestrating these events, to seeing His hand in it all, and I surrendered to His direction in how I must respond.

When God directed me to leave my profession, which after many years of work had put me in a desirable position, and to throw my lot in with Him without any notion of how that would be, I did not hesitate to make the jump. When He directed me to take a year in silence and solitude, I simply knew it was His direction, I set about doing this task, though I had never in my life spent even a single day with the object of keeping mum. In these recent years, He has directed me in this rather nomadic life, beyond my expectations of what I "should" be doing. I have followed Him implicitly, knowing that His will is automatically for the highest good of all. I know His hand has been the guiding force in these large trends in my life.

Then there is day-to-day life, so many micro-moments that are times of surrender. When the body has aches and pains and does not behave the way it should, when frustrations come up in the day, things do not go as planned, and God prompts me to do one thing when my mind thinks it should be doing something else—all of these are pin-points of surrender. By themselves, none are absolutely life-changing; however, when taken as a pattern of surrender to God, these micro-moments can most definitely make or break a spiritual life. Any one of these day-to-day moments may trigger fear, resentment, anger, or desire nature—and any one of them can veer me off track from my sadhana-spiritual practice. Spiritual life means surrender in both the big events and the little ones—one strengthening the other. Some master the big decisions, but fail in the micro-moments; others do well in the day-to-day, but get tripped up by some radical change God directs. It must be all—big, little, and everything in between.

And when you are surrendered, you experience an alignment with God that transcends the events of this world; surrender gives you the direction that is true and leads you to liberation: you know when to act, when to fight for what is true, and when to observe events unfolding. In this alignment, you experience peace and an inner assurance that God is guiding you in the myriad events of your life. You know there are no accidents in life—all situations are helping to liberate you from the tyranny of attachment. Enacting a life of surrender to God inevitably leads you to complete union with Him, your eternal savior and liberator from ignorance, and you discover the truth of who, and what, you truly are.

March 2

THE MOST WONDERFUL GIFT

Yogacharya David at Grand Tetons National Park, 2016.

I remember, when I was young, thinking that when someone in their sixties passed away, "Well of course, they are old." How times change my perspective! Touching the fabric of eternity, 64, 100, or 1,000 years seems but a blink. I stand on the brink of timelessness, and from that perspective, I am, and we are all, eternally at the beginning. It is exciting, enthralling, and propelling to think of all that can be explored, all the ways we might serve—everything that God has for each one of us, as His life unfolds before us.

While the body goes through certain changes as the miles pile up, it does not change the ever-new Joy of God-experience.

Master described his conversation with the fully realized master Swami Pranabananda, the saint with two bodies:[12]

> The body of Pranabananda, which had appeared so well and strong during my amazing first visit to him in Benares, now showed definite aging, though his posture was still admirably erect. "Swamiji," I inquired, looking straight into his eyes, "please tell me the truth: Aren't you feeling the advance of age? As the body is weakening, are your perceptions of God suffering any diminution?" He smiled angelically. "The Beloved is more than ever with me now." His complete conviction overwhelmed my mind and soul. He went on, "I am still enjoying the two pensions—one from Bhagabati here, and one from above." Pointing his finger heavenward, the saint fell into an ecstasy, his face lit with a divine glow—an ample answer to my question.

And I can truly say, God is more than ever with me now.

I have received many emails and birthday cards from around the world, and it brings to mind the most wonderful gift of my life: knowing that we share this time on the earth in order that all of us can go to God together. In my younger days, I spent much of my spiritual journey on my own. Even after meeting my beloved Guru, it was a few years before I got to know the wonderful souls who were with Mother. Before Mother's talk, we came in silently and sat to meditate. Afterward, I would sit wrapped in her uplifting power, not wanting to lose any of it. After others had hugged Mother, I would stand in line, and once hugged, I would head for my car. As God would have it, I did not live in the Seattle area, so I drove three hours each way to see Mother through some of those years. I remember driving west towards Seattle, and when I came

---

12   *Autobiography of a Yogi* (p. 246).

to Lake Washington, I could feel Mother's ambiance—an aura of spiritual power and presence that surrounded Seattle. I chanted God's name, and faithfully practiced Kriya, but remained without many kindred spirits with which to share this path. One virtue of this isolation: I was aware of my inner spiritual connection with Mother, which was independent of others. It was a deep bond that transcended time and space, and what others said or did.

However, with time, close spiritual connections were created—bonds of hearts and souls. Even though God has taken me on this wanderer's life for now, I feel that powerful connection in God with you, even as I felt it with Mother. Time, space, age, circumstances in life, all this fades into a muted background, and what stands crystal clear is my union with God, and with all dear friends.

Sri Yukteswarji said in his *Holy Science* that God fulfills all of the heart's desires. I can attest to this truth.

In the fullness of this heart, overflowing with the Divine Presence, I write these words: From this heart may that same love, power, and light flood out over all time and space, and touch your heart and soul—may you feel the same greatness and timelessness of Spirit in our Infinite Beloved that I feel now.

March 7

Plugging In

Paramhansa Yogananda: Picture taken shortly
before Master's Mahasamadhi—*The Last Smile*, 1952.

I t was on March 7th that Master chose to leave his body while
addressing a large crowd, speaking of the unique relationship
of India and America, and concluding with his poem, *My India*.[13]
1952 was the year, and its events can seem long ago—out of sight
and mind. Yet, all lives continue to resonate down through time,
and that is even more true for such a greatly realized soul as our
dear Master.

---

13   https://aumamen.com/topic/my-india-a-poem-by-paramahansa-yogananda

Spiritual masters continue to be inspirations for generations, even millennia, after an incarnation. Sometimes this is due to organizations that keep the masters in the collective consciousness, but even more relevant is the fact that having become established in eternal Life, a true master's grace can communicate itself to a sincere devotee throughout all time, and without regard for spatial distance.

Think of electricity coming from some great power source, and through a series of transmission lines, it comes into your home, to a plug-in near you. However, even though the flowing electricity is right next to you, you still need to plug into the socket and have an implement that can take advantage of its power. And this is how it is with knowing God and His great spiritual masters. The *electricity* of their grace is ever flowing to us; in fact, it is all around us, but only if we *plug in,* and have the capacity of utilizing that flow of spiritual power, can it really make a difference in our lives.

Prayer, meditation, and deep God-remembrance are the *plugging in*, and depending upon the capacity of the instrument (of your body, mind, and soul), you may make use of that Grace. A small instrument will perhaps manifest a little light, and will occasionally perform some small selfless act of service. A greater instrument will brightly illumine a room, and be in the saddle of service to God, but that service is mixed with self-interest. Then, there will be those who bring light to the whole world, those who are perfectly surrendered servants to the Almighty.

What sort of instrument was Master? Master's mother related to him that even from his birth, the perfect master, Lahiri Mahasaya had made a tremendous prediction:

> I first knew your destined path when you were but a babe in my arms. I carried you then to the home of my guru in Benares. Almost hidden behind a throng of disciples, I could barely see Lahiri Mahasaya as he sat in

deep meditation. While I patted you, I was praying that the great guru take notice and bestow a blessing. As my silent devotional demand grew in intensity, he opened his eyes and beckoned me to approach. The others made a way for me; I bowed at the sacred feet. My master seated you on his lap, placing his hand on your forehead by way of spiritually baptizing you. 'Little mother, thy son will be a yogi. As a spiritual engine, he will carry many souls to God's kingdom.' My heart leaped with joy to find my secret prayer granted by the omniscient guru. Shortly before your birth, he had told me you would follow his path.[14]

Of course, the great master's prediction bore fruit. Master *plugged into God*, and, like a great steam engine, he helped so many others to do the same—according to their capacity and their willingness. Mother Hamilton was one of the greatest of these sincere ones, coming with incredible capacity. Mother describes a moment of heartfelt surrender to her Master after his passing. Master's body had been kept in his room, and after a night of staying with his body, Mother recalls:

On the morning that they were going to take him from his room, he was laid out on the bed. He didn't have any shoes on. He had little blue socks. He was beautifully formed. His hands, his feet were perfect. I was all alone in the room with him for the moment. And I had been so glued to him, so attached to him, my love for him was so great that it extended beyond human comprehension, and my loss was indeed terrible. So, I knelt at his feet and put my head on first one foot and then the other. As I

---

14   *Autobiography of a Yogi* (p. 19).

held my head there, I prayed with everything I had in me that God would take me, would lift me up and use me to even some small degree of the way that He had used my Master, to take God's children to Him. And as I knelt there—and this is the truth as I stand before you, and God knows it—all of a sudden, from these feet came a charge of electricity that went right through the center of my head, as though he had known—that he was consciously in that body yet.

New generations have come since Master and Mother's passings, and the power of their message continues as mightily as ever; "Come, follow me!" Let us be inspired by Master and Mother's lives, let us plug into the universal current that God is constantly sending out to this vast creation. Know that the only limit is our willingness and our growing capacity. Let us link our consciousness onto the powerful engine of Master through reading his words, thinking upon him, and meditating upon the endless divinity that animated him in life; when we merge into him, we merge into the same Infinite Spirit he loved so much. God bless Master, and God bless the Work he came to do—to awaken all of us, all of creation to the Presence of our most perfect Creator.

March 10

Sri Yukteswar's Body Buried: His Spirit, Never!

Yogacharya David seated in Sri Yukteswarji's
Samadhi Temple, Puri, India, 1999.

It was on March 10 that Master and other disciples buried Sri Yukteswarji after he had attained Mahasamadhi on March 9, 1936. The delay of one day (in India bodies are, many times, dealt with on the same day as their death) was due to Master steaming by locomotive from Calcutta to Puri. Sri Yukteswarji had cabled Master to come right away, but Master had some things to finish and delayed coming—he was not there for his guru's

Mahasamadhi. This was something that Master had a very hard time forgiving himself for; he finally found resolution when Sri Yukteswarji resurrected himself to Master months later in distant Bombay.

In India, most corpses are publicly cremated as a rite of purification very soon following death. However, young children and swamis, considered already pure, are therefore either buried, or swaddled in cloth, and put into a holy river. Sri Yukteswarji was buried, seated in full lotus posture. When I was at Sri Yukteswarji's seaside hermitage in Puri, there was a peculiar picture up on the wall of the Bhajan Hall. It was strange, and I stared at it not quite comprehending. I suddenly realized that the great master was seated in meditation posture, Master and another disciple each had a hand on either of his two shoulders, holding him up. Sri Yukteswarji had already fled the body, no longer inhabiting that form, but he was sitting up in the midst of devotees. This picture took a bit of time for me to understand. It was shocking by our Western standards—but a powerful picture.

Master designed a Samadhi Temple to be constructed over the site where Sri Yukteswarji's body was put to rest. As with other traditions around the world, the bones of a saint are considered holy and are to be revered. This has, interestingly, sometimes led to fights between disciples and communities as to where the remains would find a home. This "spiritual materialism" was sometimes driven by pride of ownership, but also, a community could become wealthy as a pilgrimage site. Despite these pedestrian motives that sometimes surround the body of a great saint, there is no doubt as to the uplifting power that comes from the remains of a realized master.

I have experienced the power of the remnants of divine personalities: Lahiri Mahasaya's in Haridwar, Master's at Forest Lawn, Mother Hamilton's in The Rose Garden at Floral Hills, Papa's bones in the Bhajan Hall, Anandamayi Ma's in Kankhal, Meher

Baba's in Meherabad, Sai Baba's in Shirdi, to name some—and, of course, Sri Yukteswarji's in Puri.

My first darshan of the Puri Samadhi Temple came in 1998, when on pilgrimage there with Swami Vishwananda, Larry, Cate, and Phyllisji.[15] It was thrilling to enter the grounds and to walk in that ashram hallowed by both Sri Yukteswarji and Master. The doors to the Samadhi Temple were unlocked by the swami; we entered and sat in meditation posture. Indeed, it was powerful, uplifting, and even transforming. Swami Vishwananda was obviously moved, more deeply than I had observed at any other pilgrimage spot to which we went. We all felt the Samadhi Temple's uplifting power.

Since that darshan, I saw Sri Yukteswarji in a brand-new light. Through Master's descriptions, Sri Yukteswar often came across as stern, uncompromising in principle, and critical. Of course, Master was in training under Sri Yukteswarji and being prepared for a very difficult and powerful mission in the West; Sri Yukteswarji played a grounding role in Master's life. Beforehand, I definitely had the feeling that this great God-man, while he possessed a tremendous sense of humor, would be difficult to be around. However, with my experience in his Samadhi Temple, I came to know his unalloyed joy and sweetness of spirit! This came as a revelation, and very unexpectedly.

After our meditation, we walked the grounds of the Karar Ashram, and then the doors of the master's bedroom were unlocked, and we were given the opportunity to have its darshan. Even though the room was not well kept, dusty, with stacks of newspapers on the floor, the power of that room, with its simple wooden bed and very few items—but my, what a powerful vibration fills that room. We never wanted to leave!

---

15   Read a further description in *My Spiritual India* available through www.crossandlotus.com

I reflected on my surprising discovery of Sri Yukteswarji's unbounded joy on the spot where he was buried. My mind was directed to Master's description from *The Autobiography of a Yogi*, The Resurrection of Sri Yukteswar:

"I have now told you, Yogananda, the truths of my life, death, and resurrection. Grieve not for me; rather, broadcast everywhere the story of my resurrection from the God-dreamed earth of men to another God-dreamed planet of astrally garbed souls! New hope will be infused into the hearts of misery-mad, death-fearing dreamers of the world." "Yes, Master!" How willingly would I share with others my joy at his resurrection! "On earth my standards were uncomfortably high, unsuited to the natures of most men. Often, I scolded you more than I should have. You passed my test; your love shone through the clouds of all reprimands." He added tenderly, "I have also come today to tell you: Never again shall I wear the stern gaze of censure. I shall scold you no more." How much I had missed the chastisements of my great guru! Each one had been a guardian angel of protection. "Dearest Master! Rebuke me a million million times—do scold me now!" "I shall chide you no more." His divine voice was grave, yet with an undercurrent of laughter. "You and I shall smile together, so long as our two forms appear different in the maya-dream of God. Finally, we shall merge as one in the Cosmic Beloved; our smiles shall be His smile, our unified song of joy vibrating throughout eternity to be broadcast to God-tuned souls!"[16]

---

16   *The Autobiography of a Yogi* (p. 415).

Something in the expressional nature of Sri Yukteswarji changed after his passing—"Never again shall I wear the stern gaze of censure . . . our smiles shall be His smile, our unified song of joy vibrating throughout eternity to be broadcast to God-tuned souls!" I now had firsthand experience of his joy—unexpectedly, surprisingly, and wonderfully real. And since that experience at his Samadhi Temple in Puri almost twenty years ago, Sri Yukteswarji now stands not only as a symbol and a reality of uncompromising clarity in regards to wisdom and truth, but as an effervescent bubbling up of pure and ever-new joy. On this day of remembrance, may his light of wisdom and divine joy be broadcast to God-tuned souls everywhere.

March 15

ALL CONTRADICTIONS RESOLVED

Sunrise where we are camped at Anza-Borrego Desert, California.

It has been fascinating to bear witness to the Omniscience of Divine Consciousness. Here, in the desert remoteness, my awareness easily crosses the time-space barrier, making it seem like nothing, and thereby communing through God-consciousness with aspirants around the globe. For many, this recent time seems to be especially packed with changes, physical challenges, and transformations.

As a result, God gives me a share of what others go through; I live the lives of all those God has brought together for this spiritual journey. I do not seek out information about others, but through the magic of Omniscience, He makes me know what I need to, and very often adds a load onto me from another's life as well. It can be a load sharing of physical pain, emotional distress, or out-of-harmony thinking. God will also spontaneously pour His power through this form—I feel it go out to individuals, families/groups, and out to the world as a whole. As I say, it is fascinating to observe what Divine Intelligence and Power do in and around this form.

From an early age, and into adulthood, I worked on farms, and at other physical labor, played sports, and engaged in other physical activities. Through training for sports and hard work, the body was taken to the limits of endurance and pain. This was, as it turned out, an excellent primer for what God puts this form through now on a daily basis. One of the specialties of God, in my case, is to channel tremendous power through this form—it is wonderful, blissful, painful, and requires total surrender. An irony is that there is little life-force given for the maintenance of this body; so, at times, just moving from one part of a room to another is all I can muster. Other times, the switch is flicked on, and I have "normal" life-energy flowing through this body and I can walk and work in a completely normal way.

The other day, Carla and I were out for a walk. This can be a rare phenomenon for me at times. It was an act of pure will to keep going, but I was managing. Then we came to a slight incline; I stopped several times to catch my breath and gather a bit more life-energy. It was reminiscent of when I was extremely anemic—when the doctor said he was surprised I was able to walk into the emergency room. This incident made us both wonder, could this be anemia again? The next day I told God, "You need to prove this is not anemia." Later that day, I felt I could take a walk. Carla and I headed out over the desert. I walked so fast that Carla had to trot at times to keep up. All was well, and the next day, even though for much of the day I could not move that much,

I had another vigorous walk. The ability for movement never felt so good.

There is a primary difference in all that God puts me through, from the earlier "training" in my youth of hard physical work and training in sports, until today. Today, God's Presence is tangibly with me, actually embedded in all He puts me through. Pain and bliss are intermingled, intense pressure, and His Presence, go hand in hand; life-less-ness in the body, and tremendous shakti-power, occur simultaneously—even though God's remarkable power pours through like a full-bore train, yet the body can barely stand and move from here to there. Also, there are times when the power builds, especially when interacting directly with others, creating a backlog of pressure that threatens to break me apart, but then, when choosing, I can easily stretch out over all-space and feel an intimate connection with others (still, I am in full sympathy with yogis and mystics seeking out secluded caves).

But, this primary difference in my life today—God's living Presence—makes all the difference. It enables me to rejoice in His work, and not despair; it gives me complete knowledge that this is His will, and therefore everything He is doing is enacted for the higher good of all. It most definitely proves what Papa said, *Pain and Bliss are the same,* and what Mother said, *God is life, and all life is God.* Every experience easily fits within these truths, and all contradictions are resolved in the one unifying confluence of Spirit.

March 18

IS THERE EVIL IN THE WORLD?

Ascending through clouds of darkness—into the Light.**

M aster one time gave a talk, titled: Is There Evil in the World? He said that earlier in his life, he had rejected the notion of evil, but that experience taught him that there was real evil, that there was a satanic force in creation beyond individual acts of meanness. Of course, Papa taught that the world and all creation are God and that God is behind every action. Mother, who grew up in fear of being a sinner and in fear of the devil, wanted us to focus our attention on God, and not on sin or evil.

So, the question is—is the world nothing but God? Or, are there forces of evil and darkness acting to destroy all that is good?

Mother has helped us with this conundrum by teaching us that there are two perspectives from which to view this creation—two perspectives that remain, even for a fully God-realized master. The first is the most common, and that is the human perspective. From a human standpoint, there is evil, wrong action, and a darkness that would seek to obliterate light. The second way of knowing this creation and everything that is, is from the Divine perspective—the Universal Vision. Divine Consciousness makes us know that God is part and parcel of all that is; there is nothing that is not teeming with Divine Essence.

The human perspective is what most people live with, and what many of the scriptures describe. Dating back to the Zoroastrian, Hindu, and Judaic religions, as well as in many other sacred stories from around the world, these scriptures speak of an ongoing battle between good and evil. We are warned about evil tendencies, and to avoid them. We also see the suffering that occurs through wrong actions in our personal lives, and in the world at large. There is no doubt that the compassion of realized masters is triggered when seeing such suffering in this world.

Then, through spiritual evolution, the mind becomes purified and uplifted into a consciousness of Divinity. This transformation reveals ever-new bliss, universal love, and omnipresent light, found within and without. With this illumination, a unity of Spirit is known to be behind the alternating faces of good and evil. Even actions that are normally defined as evil are seen to eventually produce enlightenment—the suffering produced by wrong actions spurring us on to seek out God Omnipresent, and/or pay off karmic debt previously accrued. In this way, even evil is seen as part of the Divine Plan.

We are endowed with individual will; therefore, we can humanly choose good or evil. Through the consequences of our actions, we learn invaluable lessons. We see the results of evil and are eventually driven to strive to go beyond this world of opposites. In this way, we see, even from a human perspective, that all is working for the ultimate good. Through our spiritual practice, we are purified to the point that the universal vision is realized—we now actively perceive God as the sole force behind all creation. When we see actions that produce pain, our hearts bleed with compassion, and we also understand that God is truly working out His will for the highest good of all.

Human and Divine have their own ways of seeing this world, and while they are fundamentally different perspectives, they need not clash but can work together to make up the whole—a loving, compassionate, humanity working for good to overcome darkness and evil propensity, bringing forth a Divine perspective that knows that Good is the "first-born" of all creation, and even now, creation is perfect exactly as it is. Thus, the world and heaven, human and Divine, are with us in the present, and our purified vision reveals that all the world is gradually evolving toward God, and is even now is a perfect expression of the purity that is God.

Editor's Note: Paramhansa Yogananda in *The Second Coming of Christ Volume One* speaks to this perennial question of the powers of goodness and the powers of evil. Here are some of Master's thoughts on this topic:

> If one inhabits a body, he has tacitly acknowledged the duality of the world of matter. Philosophy can play an intricate word-game with truth, but what each individual has to deal with in fact is the obstinate mindset of his present state of consciousness. It is better to know the wiles of evil and the ways to combat them than to be caught unaware in blithe denial. Knowledge only, and not assertion without realization, can produce final emancipation.
>
> Man possesses the divinely given gift of free choice to tune into God's goodness, peace, and immortality. Those who use their will contrarily and act out of tune with Him, breaking His laws, are bound to suffer from the recoil of their misdeeds, according to the law of cause

and effect . . . All habits, good or bad, control and enslave the mind only after the will has allowed itself to be overcome by repeated good or evil actions born of good or evil judgment.

(Two aspects of Nature) . . . correspond to the Christian designations of Holy Ghost and Satan. The Holy Ghost in tune with Christ Consciousness creates goodness and beauty and draws all manifestation toward a symbiotic harmony and an ultimate oneness with God. Satan (from the Hebrew, literally, "the adversary") pulls outward from God into entanglement with the delusive world of matter, employing the mayic cosmic delusion to diffuse, confuse, blind, and bind.

This Satan is defined as an archangel that fell from heaven, a force fallen from the grace of attunement with the Holy Creative Vibration of God . . . The satanic aspect asserts its independence and turns from God and the heavenly realms to ply its wiles in the grossest regions of duality, contrast, inversion, oppositional states, and mortality. Because it enshrouds matter and engages man in the most deceptive confusion of mayic delusion, Jesus referred to the satanic force as a devil, a murderer, and a liar (John 8:44).

Thus, originally all Cosmic Energy, being vibrated by the Holy Ghost and Christ Intelligence, was flowing Godward, creating perfect images from astral light turned inward to reveal God. The conscious Cosmic Delusive Force (Satan), with independent power from God, saw that if the cosmic-energy manifestations of the Holy Ghost Vibration were to dissolve back into Spirit according to the divine plan, then its own separate existence would also cease. Without the Holy Vibration, there would be neither a reason for nor sustenance of the Cosmic Delusive Force. . . .

So, for his own purpose of self-perpetuation he rebelled against God . . . he manipulated the laws and principles of creation under his command to establish patterns of imperfection . . .

Therefore, it can be said that except in the absolute sense that everything is made in the one Cosmic Consciousness of God, there is no evil in the All-Perfect God. Evil resides in the Adversarial Force that maintains its realm of influence by the gross obscuration of the true God-nature of all created beings . . . Satan has conjured an ugly counterpart for every beautiful creation of God in man's body and mind, and in Nature.

God created a wondrous human form to be charged by cosmic energy, and to live in a free, unconditioned divine state; but Satan created hunger and the lure of sensory indulgence. For mental power, Satan substituted mental temptation; for the soul's wisdom, Satan contrived perplexing ignorance; for the grandeur of Nature, Satan countered with the potentialities of warfare, disease, pestilence, earthquakes, floods—a horde of disasters.

Since God gave independence to man as well as to Satan, He can free souls only with their permission and cooperation. . . . Satan thereby tries to keep human beings deluded by greed, anger, fear, desire, attachment, and ignorance; so, God uses the psychological counterparts of self-control, calmness, courage, satisfaction, unattached divine love, and wisdom to bring man to His Divine Kingdom.

Jesus, in lifting himself from the Holy Ghost state of omnipresent Cosmic Vibration and its Christ Consciousness immanent in vibratory space into oneness with Cosmic Consciousness—the transcendental, vibrationless God the Father as well as the Father's reflection as the universal Christ Consciousness—experienced a matter-ward pull of cosmic delusion, a reminder of confining, limiting, human habits of incarnations. The Divine Spirit had led Jesus into the silence of the wilderness to be tested, to see if his Christ Consciousness could be retained despite the deluding influence of all mortal memories.

The ordinary man's encounter with "The Tempter" is primarily as subjective ideas subtly luring him through prenatal and postnatal bad habits and the come-hither attraction of his material environment. To obstruct the highly advanced, Satan may take objective form and use vibratory voices in his desperate last attempt to dissuade the Godward-fleeing master...

Every time man is tempted to do wrong, he should remind himself that it is not his subjective mind alone that is tempting him, but also objective Satan. He should adamantly refuse to cooperate with the Evil One who would destroy him. That is why Jesus said, "Get thee behind me Satan" when the Evil Force showed him kingdoms of temporal glory, which could be his if he worshiped delusion . . . By emerging victorious from temptation, he (Jesus) is a shining example for all souls struggling to regain their divine sonhood.[17]

Finally, my brethren, be strong in the Lord, and in the power of His might. Put on the whole armor of God, that ye may be able to stand against the wiles of the devil. For

---

17   *The Second Coming of Christ: Volume One* (pp. 134–159). Editors Note: Paramhansa Yogananda explains this theme well in several chapters of this volume. From a Vedic-Eastern perspective, much has been written about the sophisticated, disruptive, multilayered forces of ignorance and degradation. Rudolf Steiner, a wise Elder from the West, speaks of two quite different forces that create chaos and angst, the Satanic (or Ahrimanic), and the Luciferic in *The Incarnation of Ahriman*. Steiner, as does Master, discusses how complex, entrancing, and tricky evil can be, and how imperative it is that humans stay awake and vigilant.

we wrestle not against the flesh and blood, but against principalities, against powers, against the rulers of the darkness in this world (Ephesians 6:10–12).

March 25

RIGHT ACTION

Shiva gives the heavenly weapon Pashupatastra to Arjuna**

There must be a foundation, firm principles, on which to build our spiritual practice: tenets that can lead us to freedom and not into further bondage of the ego, the things of the senses, and this world. In the East, this foundation is called dharma, sometimes defined as "right action," such as what is spelled out in the ten commandments. But there is also inborn dharma—seen as transcendent truth. By knowing this truth, we will be automatically guided to right action—or to living in conscious harmony with God. Attunement with dharma leads to spiritual freedom; ignoring or going against those principles of ultimate truth leads to wrong actions, and further binds the soul in ignorance and darkness.

Spiritual teachers and sacred practices are here to liberate us from darkness and ignorance—the word "guru" means from darkness to light. Dharma has become encoded into spiritual principles and laws, but just as a lawyer can look for loopholes without sincerity, those principles can be used for bad ends. For instance, I have seen people "just telling the truth," but they are actually using facts like a bludgeon, to hurt and maim. For dharma to be fulfilled, truth must be combined with compassion, love, and ahimsa (do no harm).

In the spiritual field, even as in the fields of politics, business, and psychology, there are those who come along who seek to rewrite the rules of right action, either through their public teachings, or their private behavior. It never turns out well. These "false prophets" become a law unto themselves, and though they begin with a promise of freedom and liberation, they, and those around them, soon become ensnared in their own ignorance.

Some devotees let me know about a documentary of a spiritual teacher named Rajneesh, later called Osho—a teacher from India who came to America and was expedited back out some eight years later. We have watched three episodes of the five-part series and have found it to be well done. The people who were actually involved on both sides of the issue were interviewed. It is a disturbing story of actual events and comes as a cautionary tale.

Rajneesh came on the scene when many Westerners were looking for alternatives to their own culture. He combined some traditional teachings of India (he had been a professor of philosophy in India), along with what he termed to be "revolutionary methods" for awakening. He taught followers to access their deepest emotions and desires, act them out, then find calm in meditation—this he called a transmutation of the energy.

In theory, and rightly understood, there is some element of truth in this. For instance, a married couple can enjoy a sexual union that is transformed by love, caring, commitment, and spiritual attunement, which transmutes a purely physical act into one of pure love and spiritual union. Or, anger may be channeled in a safe environment, where ground rules are understood, and individuals can achieve the catharsis of deeply-held feelings.

However, in practice, in the groups led by Rajneesh, anger was acted out in group shouting matches and brawling, which sometimes resulted in broken bones and injuries. Then, group sex was engaged in, and traditional marriage was dismissed as irrelevant and was defined however two or more chose to define it for as long as they wanted to do so.

Being a sannyasin was completely stood on its head, with free sexual expression without restraint, and being wealthy was encouraged for his "sannyasins." Wearing the colors of red, orange, and purple gave recognition of being such a sannyasin. These "principles" attracted many people of the time, a seeming release from old rules, promising a new freedom. I worked at the same agency with some who wore these "sannyasin" colors, but they worked at another facility, and I did not have an opportunity to speak with them while they worked there.

Rajneesh himself was not averse to money, or the finer things in life. One could not own too many Royal Royces: he had twenty or more and wore a million-dollar diamond watch. You get the picture. On the other side, there were interviews with those who were profoundly affected, and whose lives were changed by Rajneesh. The fact that he was irreverent, revolutionary, and threw out the old rules was attractive to many. But with the rules thrown out, greed and ungoverned avarice arose, and the unraveling was inevitable—like watching a head-on train wreck in slow motion.

The "ashram" in eastern Oregon had a disco and a casino. Rajneesh was not giving talks, said to be in silence, but took calls from his Rolls Royce dealer when ordering new cars. He was reported to be hooked on drugs. Alcohol was served to the "sannyasins" every day—it was painful to see words like ashram and sannyasin turned on their heads and used in opposite ways to their true meanings.

It can be tempting to think the spiritual path does not require self-discipline, rules of conduct, sacrifice, hard work, and death of the ego—the idea that anything goes can definitely be tempting to the ego-mind. Rajneesh came to the point where he privately said he admired Hitler, and that his opponents in Oregon would need to die. Ah, so painful to see.

And the lesson for me: Thank you, Mother! Thank you for standing against the tide of free love/ casual sex, recreational use of drugs and alcohol, and smoking. Thank you for upholding the eternal values of dharma. Observing my own life, and observing the lives of others, has only reinforced that necessity for living by these eternal values. Truly, there are traditions that need to be questioned, and when found faulty, to be done away with. But this should not be a wild foray into hedonism, expediency for the ego, and definitely not living by the creed: "If it feels good, do it." Such license for behavior promises easy freedom but ends in karmic jail.

So, thank you, Mother, Guru-lineage, and true saints and spiritual masters, for showing us the Way—for being the examples of right action. It is not the easy path of no rules, but it is the path that leads to freedom. My eternal gratitude to the blessed Guru and Guru-lineage for being the Way for all of us.

✳   ✳   ✳

Travel Note: We are driving north; actually, Carla is driving right now while I am sending this out. We look forward to seeing everyone for Easter! With loving pronams.

March 30

PERFECT LOVE

Figure of Christ, painting by Heinrich Hofmann, 1884.**

Jesus, the great Master, came with a unifying message for all humankind: We are all children of the one Father-God, and through the perfection of our love for our Father, and for all His children everywhere, we might rise up in oneness with Him. As we approach the anniversary of His flawless gift of surrender and transformation, we can meditate upon His life and message, and thus be transformed into His perfect likeness.

How greatly the Master loves all humanity. There are none outside of His **love**, and we should be exactly as He, in all respects. To Him, there are no untouchables, no one who cannot be absolved of sins—no matter how badly that one has behaved, when one sincerely turns from wickedness and seeks the ever-pure light. In a world that divides humanity into those who are chosen and others who are outsiders, the Master recognizes no such barriers. Those who love, and act on that love, are His proclaimed brothers and sisters.

And He has spoken, nothing but the **truth**, even when it cost Him everything. He taught in small groups, He spoke to multitudes, and He never wavered—even when threatened with torture and death. Because Jesus has always spoken the truth, those who are sincere recognize the power of what He says, even when they do not always understand His true meaning. Those closest to Him are not immune to his sharp corrections, the keen sword of wisdom that slices ego to the bone—unrelenting, ever vigilant, finely tuned to the verities of his Heavenly Father. We too should follow his example and speak loving truth without compromise.

Although Jesus is the Master of the ages, still He demanded nothing for himself. He did not need to be worshiped, He did not even want word to go out of his healings; rather, He instructed those who experienced his grace to worship their mutual Heavenly Father. **Humility** was his watchword, and though he spoke with great power and authority, still Jesus knew it is not I, but my Heavenly Father who does all things through me (John 14:10, adapted). In our quest to emulate Him, we too should manifest only the Father; let His light so shine through our thoughts, words, and actions, so that all will be inspired to seek out our Heavenly Father.

Good Friday is the apex of his—and humanity's—existence. In the Garden of Gethsemane came his ultimate **surrender**. Although throughout his life he lived in surrender to His Heavenly Father, on that fated, darkest night, he found himself in the depths of despair—his angst was a moment of tremendous spiritual crisis at which time he gave all that he had and all that he was. It was then that the arrogance of Adam and Eve was overturned; in that moment, he triggered the Mystical Crucifixion in which all separation from God was to be effaced; no longer would there be any sense of self, but only oneness—only God. We too must surrender our all; we too must traverse Gardens—from the barred gates of Eden to Gethsemane's "Not my will, but Thine" (Luke 22:42) from being a separated human, to ultimate Divine Union.

From the three stages of the **crucifixion,** we must follow another three for the **resurrection**. "Touch me not," means we must rise—and not fall back into separateness by the temptations of body or mind. Continued surrender, and a perfect love for God, must be enacted—eschewing all attachment to this world until the work is complete. To lift the chosen twelve up the spinal ladder of perfection is a tremendous work, a total work, that must not suffer delusion's grip at any time—though test after test is still to come.

The Master's life is one of **perfect love in God**, and the resurrection must be seen in its transcendental perfection. How rare and beautiful is that final journey. And how greatly the Master beckons to us, prods us, even pleads with us to follow—so that we may know what he knows, experience what he experiences, and be what he has become.

Surely, his greatness knows no end and endures for all eternity. His mystery is that **in his humanity, we see the all-pervasive shining Divinity**. Oh, children of the Infinite! He is calling to us, and we must listen—for he is awake, and he is seeking to rouse us from our dreaming delusion. His life is our life; his journey is ours when we emulate him in every detail. Let us pick up our cross Oh blessed ones, follow him, and be transformed from the *son of man* to the *Son of God*—know him as our very Self. Let us make this Good Friday and Easter an inspiration for our own perfect love.

April 1

RESURRECTION DAY

Empty tomb with light streaming in.**

oday, we celebrate Resurrection Day, the day that Lord Jesus made his physical body come to radiant life after being horribly crucified. Since then, there has been much said and written about the resurrection by those who believe in the Second Coming of the Christ. However, why should so much be made of resurrecting the body alone?

The word resurrection has interesting Latin roots. It comes from the verb rego, to make straight, plus the preposition of sub, or under; then surrectum, to rise. Put together, it is "a straight-ening from under again." Take the root meaning: to take what is under, make it straight, and to arise; this instruction can be perfectly applied to sadhana, spiritual practice. To take the lower impulses of the ego-mind, and make it straight through God-remembrance, so that consciousness can rise into spiritual union with our Heavenly Father. Rather than focusing on the body alone as resurrected, this way of understanding the word entails the transformation of the whole inner person. Jesus, the son of man, becomes Jesus Anointed—the Son of God. And in his wake, we, those he commanded, are to follow in his footsteps. For the Master said, "And he who does not take his cross and followeth me, is not worthy of me" (Matthew 10:38).

The spring equinox reminds us to celebrate the resurrection, as it is wonderfully symbolic of the arisen consciousness. Locally, the daffodils are bursting into bloom. Like so many rays of golden suns, life is returning after slumbering in winter, seeds burst their bonds, and branches reach out for the light—new life, new hope, a renewed world. As we meditate upon this miracle of nature, let us know that an even greater miracle is promised within—the resurrection of Divine Consciousness, that we may know our Heavenly Father in truth and reality.

So let us pick up our cross, the body, and follow after our Lord, to meditate deeply upon that inner Light that is seeking to draw us unto itself. This story is not a fairy tale, nor is it an event that only took place two thousand years ago. The resurrection is a living legacy from all those who have gone before us and have gained their resurrected Divine Consciousness—and this resurrection is seeking to do so in you now.

Blessings to you my dear ones on this Resurrection Day, a blessed day for a new life in Christ Consciousness.

April 4

THREE TIMES, HE FELL

Christ in Gethsemane, painting by Heinrich Hofmann, 1886.**

I am cradled in the Divine Presence, wrapped in His Bliss in a happy hangover after Easter. I think over the weekend's activities of celebrating the Divine Resurrection: the kirtan at Jerry and Lois's, the Easter Service, the potluck, and seeing so many devotees of God glowing in His Light, and the little ones hunting Easter eggs, then watching Zeffirelli's *Jesus of Nazareth*[18]—starting with the powerful scene of Jesus raising Lazarus from the dead

---

18   *Jesus of Nazareth.* (1972). Directed by Franco Zeffireli. ITC Entertainment, RAI.

and ending with the Christ's resurrection. After the disciples had dispersed during the Master's arrest, they gathered again after the crucifixion. Peter, talking about his denial of Jesus, said, "We all abandoned him! But he has forgiven us, forgiven us all." A statement of such pure compassionate truth.

This morning, God has been talking to me—it is very interesting, the way He does this. In the stillness of my mind, a teaching flows in as pure thought. This stream of Consciousness is clearly from above, and I am but a witness to the thoughts, pictures, and wordless-words that manifest on my mental screen. It is an intimate union, and He tells me the most wonderful things. His expositions are often about the path to realization. With a fine scalpel of discernment, He cuts away gross and subtle falsehoods, those things that can derail us, and He reveals the Way.

This morning, the Lord picked up on a theme He had spoken about on Sunday—Jesus fell three times while carrying his cross—or the body—up the hill of Golgotha—meaning Hill of the Skull (i.e., ascending spinal consciousness to the higher centers of the brain). Of course, this story of Christ from two thousand years ago is conveying what happens in everyone's spiritual journey to complete realization. When we are put through the Mystical Crucifixion, we are tempted, and tempted hard, even as Peter was in his fearful denial of Jesus. In that temptation, we may fall—three times, the Christ fell, and he was born an incarnation of Divinity.

Mother and Master also made mistakes on the way up, and this is true with all ascending souls. We have all fallen short of the goal of perfection. "For all have sinned, and come short of the glory of God" (Romans 3:23). And here, we tread a fine line when talking about the ways great masters fell during their upward journey to spiritual perfection. There are those who are too apt to see their spiritual heroes as being too good to make mistakes, and hence, any so-called imperfection threatens the picture-perfect image they have created of a master—if they encounter a flaw, their entire worldview is threatened. And then there are those who glory in their fellow human's imperfection. Thus, we have tabloids appealing to the voyeur who gets a charge from tantalizing details.

To have a realistic view of the spiritual path upon which we tread, we must know that: "Yes, we can fall," and, "Yes, we can recover." None of us would like to be defined by a past when we were not at our best; we must have the freedom to learn and grow from our experiences. And while we need not shamefully hide away unlovely truths about ourselves, we should also not get overly fixated on the faults or shortcomings of another. This is the razor's edge, to know the whole truth of a soul's journey, and not get hung up on something negative when the bigger picture reveals a soul ascending beyond those falls on their way to spiritual perfection.

"So," one may ask, "how do I discriminate between true spiritual masters who made missteps on the way up, and those who portray themselves as spiritual adepts, but in reality, they are hypocrites, wolves in sheep's clothing?" For that, we carefully observe—what happens next? When one falls, then tries to cover it up, continues to stumble from one fall to another, and casts the blame on others while not doing the hard work to change oneself—that is the very definition of a hypocrite. When, on the other hand, following a fall, the aspirant continues to strive for God; through repentance, or turning away from temptation, the sincere seeker makes reparations where possible, and through intense sadhana, deepens meditation, humility, and surrender—thereby coming into contact with the fabric of God's Being, and is renewed in Spirit—then that one grows, and in time, he or she is perfected. A humble tenacity that never gives up, and never gives in, is a sign of a true, aspiring spiritual master.

A boxer may get knocked down with a terrific blow. But then comes that critical moment, does he get back up or stay down on the mat? Even though the athlete may go down, the champion gets back up, shakes off the blinding pain, and continues—and may very well go on to win. The sign of a champion athlete is not that he or she never stumbles, but that he or she never gives up. So, too, for the spiritual champion. One may take a knock, but what comes next is not to grovel in the mud and give up, but to pick oneself up, wash the muck off, heal the wounds, and get right back on the path to Self-realization.

As our dear Lahiri Baba prescribed—striving, striving, striving, behold, one day the Goal! There is a saying that, "Rust never sleeps," so, too, with ignorance; it never goes on vacation. Every day proves the necessity for striving in our spiritual practice. Ego's default is to seek out the muddy puddles of ignorance—where it feels at home. However, there comes a day, through ever-deepening practice, when we feel more at home swimming in the Ocean of Light and Bliss, inwardly attuned to Spirit—this, then, is the *new normal*.

I have put to words here what my Lord was speaking to me wordlessly. May this teaching be one for healing the past and renewing hope for what is to come—may it deepen your understanding of your own journey, and provide you with compassionate clarity for the lives of others. As an aspirant, you must work and strive with all of your heart, mind, and will; moreover, you must hold the highest standards ever before you. Attaining the supreme truth reveals that real discernment is always saturated with compassion for all those who strive. We are all on our journey, and everyone must return to the Source from which we have come. The wise make straight the way of the Lord; the wise do not look left or right, but ever strive and ultimately achieve the purity of the highest realization.

April 8

His Joy-Filled Prisoner and Slave

Be a Light unto this world.**

I am being held prisoner. I should make it clear that I voluntarily became God's slave some time ago—in fact, I worked hard to do so. Even though my slavery and my imprisonment are entirely with my consent, by putting God first and making it clear, "Not my will, but thine, be done" (Luke 22:42), I have deliberately placed myself in this situation where my little human desires are routinely overwritten by God's.

It is true that I have not even the smallest wish (well, sometimes maybe the smallest wish) to not be His slave. But it is not a wish to not be His instrument, it is only the groan of a bridge over which a heavy load is being driven, being stretched to the utmost of human limits. Fortunately, I do not depend on my human strength for the work He has me do.

Now, it may all sound a bit vague, what this work is, and in truth, it can be very difficult to describe. At any hour of the day, and all through the day, God uses this human instrument as His conduit of power, bliss, and light. He also puts loads upon this human frame of illness, as well as mental and emotional disharmony—in short, any part of the human condition this world finds itself in. Since I experience His grace along with what he gives me to bear, there is always His power for strength, and the certain knowledge that it is all He. This grace makes all the difference; without His constant sustenance, the human element could not last a second.

It is the most fascinating life imaginable, and in one day, even one hour is not like another. Because of His insistence in recent years, I spend many days withdrawn from human interactions. There are exceptions to this, such as this past Easter weekend, but He makes it abundantly clear when those limits are reached.

Being His slave is perfect, but when He has me disappoint others, I must surrender that disappointment at His feet. This weekend, I was not able to attend a House Blessing, and that became one of those points of surrender, surrendering my little human desire to be there at the feet of God. I am certain that Reverend Jill did a beautiful job leading the House Blessing—so I let it go. In my absence, I sent a letter to Sarah and all attendees, within which I closed with a blessing. I am passing that blessing on to you—that God and Gurus may richly bless you. And, if it be your sweet will, you too may enjoy being a slave to the Almighty, our Infinite Beloved.

BLESSING FOR THE HOUSEHOLDER YOGI

Bless you and your home; make it a sanctuary that is a witness and a support to your aspiring spirit. As the petals of God-experiences unfold in your receptive soul, may they reveal the flower of Self-realization that lights your whole Being, your entire home, and fills all the world with His eternal splendor. Ever in God, Christ, Gurus.

April 13

ALL IN HARMONIOUS RHYTHM WITH GOD, CHRIST, AND GURU

Guru Disciple—Eternal Friendship: Paramhansa
Yogananda with Rajasi Janakananda, 1938.

I have been immersed in the sea of Mother Hamilton, swimming in her spiritual waters, as I work with her talks in preparing them for publication. We are making nice progress, but there is much to do before we are ready to go to press. In the meantime, as I work with transcripts of Mother's talks, her words, thoughts, and her spirit are so very much present, in and all around me. Oh, what a treasure we have in Mother.

And not just Mother, but how the currents of her life intermingled with Master Yogananda, Sister Gyanamata, Rajasi, and others.

Although Gyanamata and Rajasi have not been so well known, what tremendous spiritual personalities they are. Gyanamata—Mother of Wisdom through Devotion—and Mother were closely connected in their Seattle days, and they continued in their friendship after Sister Gyanamata moved down to the Mount Washington headquarters and played such an important part in Master's work.

A brilliant woman, with the social status of being married to the dean of the University of Washington's school of law, Gyanamata had the heart of a bhakta—with a total and complete devotion to Master. In any gathering, she never turned her back on Master, feeling that it would be disrespectful to him. Even though she suffered some grievous illnesses, if Master came to see her, she insisted on getting up from her sickbed to honor him. Under a large picture she had of Master, like Mother's lithograph of Master, Gyanamata had the words *God Alone* as her motto written under it. And, she lived it—with all of her heart, mind, and soul.

And Rajasi, what a soul. A brilliant man, he had a "Midas Touch" when it came to business—starting with nothing, he became a multi-millionaire in his young thirties (translate that to billionaire in today's value). Yet, this titan of business was Master's little boy. Such a loving, affectionate, relationship they held for one another. Even though a great business success, before meeting Master, Rajasi could not sit still for a minute; his hands were always fidgeting, his mind racing, and he was desperately unhappy. When he attended Master's lectures for their first meeting, on the second night, he noticed his hands were still; he was feeling a great inner peace. Soon, he was established in that peace, and the strength of consciousness he had built in previous lives as a Himalayan meditating yogi came to the fore. Since his meditating spiritual life was not welcome on the home front, he went into work early, closed his office door, and deeply meditated before his workday started. He had an unshakable love and reverence for Master, but it was different in expression from Gyanamata and Master—there was an easy friendship and exchange of love between guru and disciple with Master and Rajasi.

Both Gyanamata and Rajasi were to have significant effects on Mother; both were part of her going all the way to her complete realization of God. How blessed we are to have these tremendous spiritual personalities in our lives. For, even as they were part of Mother's journey to God, so, through Mother, they become part of us as well. One thing we can observe is how unique the outward expressions of these devotees are. Yet, even accounting for their differences, go under the surface, and there you find God-joy, God-love, and God-wisdom.

Measuring spiritual beings is fundamentally different from evaluating people by worldly standards. Mother was standing next to a devotee who criticized Rajasi when he was seen being led like a child from one place to another, and others needed to tell him what to do; sometimes, he put the wrong clothes on, like wearing casual sneakers with a suit coat and pants (long before that became fashionable in some sets). Mother said, "Well, of course, when your mind is so focused upon God that you're in the tremendous ecstasy of God, you're not conscious of anything." Imagine this titan of business, so childlike in God's bliss—what humility, what surrender he had in God.

Let us take inspiration from these saints, knowing that they have walked in the same world as we, and found their freedom in the infinite Divine. Rajasi, Gyanamata, and Mother, all unique expressions of the Divine Mind, yet their hearts beat in perfect harmonious rhythm with inward attunement to God, Christ, and Gurus.

April 15

THE GREAT FRONTIER

Papa Ramdas: A fearless explorer, Anandashram, India.

A frontier is the limit or boundary of an area or nation; mentally, it is the extreme limit of understanding, and in meditation, we have a frontier, that is where we meet the limit, and we allow ourselves to surrender to God. For us to continue to make progress in deepening meditation, we must face the inner frontiers that act as resistance: resistance being the self-imposed boundaries created by the ego-mind.

The ego-mind draws a circumference around itself to define itself; it is what the ego does. The nature of the ego is to say: "This is me, and this is not me." This belief allows the ego to operate in the world according to its own comfort, and to make decisions. As a child develops, there comes a fateful day when the mind says, "mine." Small children will play a game in which they choose to keep a toy and not give it to the mother—then they will arbitrarily turn around and give it to the mother in total delight. The next step is to consider an object mine unless I sell it. Of course, this is how the world operates on a daily basis, with some being misers, and others, generous.

In India, sadhus take a vow to have no possessions and to not stay at any one place for more than three days. This discipline is to break the idea of, "this is mine," to eliminate the ego-mind. Even in a sadhu's world, as Papa humorously writes, one can find the ego-mind inserting itself. Whether it is the position in line for meals being served, or possessiveness of a lota pot for water, or even one's cloth—the sense of position or possession, can exhibit the idea of "mine" in the most subtle of ways. Papa describes how a seeming madman came into a hut he was staying in and demanded that Papa hand over, one by one, every "possession" he had—which was very little. For Papa, this madman was his beloved Ram come in this form, and he immediately took it as a test as to see whether he had any attachment to these things. Papa cheerfully handed over every item until he was down to his last cloth, one that he wore in modesty. That, too, Papa started to give, when the man suddenly changed his mind and said no, Papa could keep that. The man left, but Papa was in such a state of bliss at having this interaction with God that he merged into his infinite Beloved in samadhi and stayed that way until far into the next day. At which time he found himself surrounded by devotees who had come to see him and sat in wonder as to why Papa was reduced to wearing only one small cloth!

Your attachment to things is a small thing compared to your attachment to the boundaries of the mind. You sit in meditation, and focus on the ajna, the point between the eyebrows; you face your frontier—that which is in front of you. It may be the immediate darkness you see with closed eyes, or if your consciousness has expanded, it is the vast, but limited, sphere of consciousness. You may be in a deep state of stillness when, suddenly, thoughts about the world create waves upon the mirror-like surface of your mind.

I remember many a time in meditation when I had the sense I was dropping deeper, like going down through the thermal layers of the ocean. Suddenly, some thought would whiplash me back to the surface—some idea activated worldly awareness and took me from that wonderful state of stillness. On other occasions, I would feel uplifted, expanded, like going up in a hot air balloon. In this state of blissful expansiveness, some thought would come along and attach. I would unthinkingly reach out to the thought or memory, then the presence of that thought would weigh down the balloon, and I would descend from those heights—it was maddening.

Oh, to be present to God with no attachments, no artificial limits—no fear of infinite expansion, nor of being taken into the minute world of subatomic matter—to go anywhere God takes you, without fear or desire, is perfect freedom. Then, the active ego-mind is transformed into the witness to what is; and all that is, is Divine in origin. When your absorption in meditation transitions into activity in the world, then all sensory input is seen and felt as God living His life through His creation. You and all others, animate and so-called inanimate, are all part and parcel of one Divine Life.

A few months ago, I injured my bicep tendon. As a result, moving my arm in a certain direction overhead or behind, created a blindingly shooting pain. Pain can bring up any number of attachments to the body, resulting in fear, anger, resentment, and depression. It has long been my long practice to see pain as coming from God—the pain impulses being activated prana, life-energy, traveling at high speed through the nerves to the brain. Prana, coming from God, is nothing but God in that form—to practice allowing the pain impulse to pass through the brain and into the light, not simply to be absorbed in the brain, but affirming that the life-energy in this form is God, just as all other forms of life-energy are God. An interesting thing began to happen with the pain from this tendon area. Instead of coming as a pain impulse, with internal vision, I saw the shoulder area emit light instead of a shooting pain. God is so interesting.

When we are in the adventure of exploring God, in creation and beyond, and we challenge the frontiers of limitations, not accepting anything in life as being normal—in the sense of being absent of God—then the normal frontiers dissolve into something more, something greater, something Divine. For most of us, this is a process. However, it does not take much reflection to see the various ways in life that our minds have created barriers, even beyond our conscious intention—and that these barriers keep us separated from Sacred-awareness. To know God as bliss, wisdom, light, expansiveness, and the deep—to know Him as our all and all, in all, is real freedom, true liberation.

Let us journey together until we know, absolutely know, there is nothing but He, nothing but He. And, as our dear Swami Satchidanandaji said to do, "Dive deep, soar high."

April 19

THE ONE IMMUTABLE LAW

Waterlily in pond, Acadia National Park, Maine.**

"Work is love made visible."—KAHLIL GIBRAN

There are many forms of government, various kinds of legal systems, and methods for changing or not changing, the status quo that creates a patchwork covering the earth. Of course, the structure of government and legal systems are important; the founding fathers created a check and balance form of government so that structure would help keep things from devolving into despotism. However, whatever the form of government, legal system, and opportunities for businesses are in place, there is one immutable law that will determine the greatest happiness for the most people—the law of love. Without this guiding principle, all forms of government and legal systems are simply empty shells.

When you have a rule of law, but there is no love and compassion, then true justice will ultimately be sacrificed. When you have a government and ruling bodies, and there is no love as a guiding light, they will become corrupt, and they will not produce the greatest general good. When you have a business, and there is no love behind its intention or its practice, then its goods and services will not truly benefit society.

Love, as spoken of here, is not sentimentality, but a guiding force. When you love, you will not do things that you know will bring about harm to yourself or others. When you love, you will not act out of greed, but with integrity, evoking the principle of love for one and all. When you pass laws and regulations, you work for the highest good of all when love is your motivation.

In running a business, you might say, "I have got a business to run. I don't have time to start the day with a group hug!" And if that is your view of the kind of love I am talking about, I would agree that this is missing the mark. Love is a far more important and vital a principle than a mere show of emotionalism. Love speaks to something much more basic in you. When you go into business, of course, you must earn a profit, otherwise, the business will not be there in any capacity the next year. However, in running your business, does your service or product bring about some good? Good for the customers, good for employees, good for the community?

In dealings with customers, do you employ the *Golden Rule*, as J.C. Penney did when starting his first store: Treat your customers as you would want to be treated? The way you work with co-workers, employees, and bosses—do you treat all others the way you would want to be treated if you were in their position? The very best owners, managers, and employees do exactly this. These Golden Rule types are the kind of people you want to work for. They are the kind of workers you want in your business, and companies, and with this motto branded into their thinking, words, and actions, these are the kind of businesses you want to patronize.

When you are in a position of authority, do you set out with the intention to better the lives of people when you make decisions? This speaks to fundamental intention, and how that intention is translated into day-to-day behavior. Love considers, "What is for the highest good of all?" A policeman will take to heart the motto: "To Protect and To Serve." Yes, laws will be enforced, occasionally with force, but all behavior of the police is governed by the overriding intention: What is for the health of the community? For a judge, a county administrator, a governor, a representative, or a leader of a country: What is for the highest good of all? You may not always get it right, but your intention is unwavering. This is acting out of love—not selfishness, greed, building a petty fiefdom, and not responding to the thousand other lower motivations.

In seeking to treat the customer as you want to be treated, or administrating with the intention for the highest good of all, does not mean you gratify the demands of every person who walks through the door. First of all, you never will be able to do so. Secondly, what one individual or group wants may not truly be for the highest good of all. Love will legitimately say "No" to some—in fact, love demands the word "No" at times.

And love in service to others is not just for the good of the recipient. When you serve with love, when love flows through your thoughts, words, and actions, it blesses you. Jesus said of the great principle: As you give, so shall you receive (Luke 6:8, adapted). This does not mean every person is going to treat you with love when you love them first. What it does mean is that when your focus is on love, giving good service, speaking the truth, and offering kindness and compassion, and you do all this without expectation of receiving it in return, then you are saturated with the quality of love—because it has flowed through you, it blesses you. This is due to the nature of love that I am speaking of: it does not emanate from you; rather, it flows through you from something greater than just you.

When you are in integrity with this higher love, you run an honest, clean/clear business, and you feel the purity of that honesty—you are left without stains on your soul. You do not ever need to look over your shoulder for someone coming up behind you because you have cheated or lied to them. There is a fair exchange of money for goods or services: both giver and receiver benefit from this transaction. This clarity of purpose, this purity of action, is what you carry forward with you; it is a gift you have given to yourself, and to the world you interact with.

Every human misery can trace its roots back to a wrong motive, which results in wrong action. You punish, or reward, yourself and those around you according to the purity of your intentions. Beginning with, and carrying through with, the intention of love not only rewards you internally—it is what defines the best business practices, the best government, and the best legal system. It is not always openly displayed through talking about love, but you know when someone is acting with integrity, sincerity, and working to give the best goods and services—you naturally want to reward them with more business and recommend them to others.

Such love may not be listed on the business banner, but it is broadcast through the quality of its goods and services. Just think of a world in which each person serves all others with love—what a tremendous world that will be!

April 26

BOTH FEET IN: TRUST IN GOD

Mother Hamilton, c. 1967.**

This past weekend we had our Loon Lake Retreat—we had a tremendous time together. My only wish is that all of us could be there for satsang. The topic was a meditation on trust: trust in God. The work that aspirants did at the retreat, then additional work done as many continued their inner work during individual appointments at Maple Ridge after the retreat, was impressive. This brings me a deepening appreciation for the willingness, courage, determination, sincerity, and openness that devotees exhibit in their desire to grow in God.

All aspirants think they can do better—but the key to real progress is to ensure that both feet are put into the arena. I remember a time when I recognized that I always played it safe, never really committing myself to anything. At the time, this was due to the fact that I did not fully believe in what I was doing in the world. Then I found my spiritual path, and for the first time, I was one hundred percent committed. Yet, the old habit of having one foot in, and one foot out, of the arena was still playing a role; my sadhana was affected.

One reason for playing it safe was that, if I did not succeed (so the unconscious reasoning went), I could justify that I had not really given it my all, and thus I preserve my ego. Well, this would not do. It was not acceptable to not be fully in the game, to not commit myself heart, mind, and soul in order to realize God—my one reason for taking incarnation. This was the most important decision I have made in my life, and it has made all the difference.

There is a tendency for the ego-mind to hedge its bets, to keep a safety valve available, to not be fully committed. When I see others jump in with both feet, do the work, and make God first with everything they have, I stand in admiration and awe. I know that the results will come, that that one is standing on the cusp of something great. To meditate deeply, to serve the Infinite in all one does, to commit to using discrimination and making God first, and to love the Beloved with all one's heart, is to draw nigh to blessed Spirit.

Mother did not want a formal organization, or a church mortgage that must be paid, or committees for this and that; she wanted us to avoid these traps and distractions so we could make God our single focus. We have our marching orders; we know what we must do; now, it is a matter of giving our all, having both feet in the arena, and going all the way to becoming fully realized. It is what Mother wants for you; it is what all the great masters want for you, and it is God calling to you, *Come to Me*—with both feet in!

I bow to the commitment you make in knowing God, and to all the support you give for this work we do in His Name. Pronams.

April 29

DIVING DEEP

Swami Ramdas (Papa): A diver of the deep.

Life is not what you think. A few years ago, I had the specter of death following me for a year. That specter culminated in severe anemia that led to a diagnosis of tumors. This led to several operations, then treatments, and then recovery from the treatments. Recovery then led to another stage, that is, the past few years of remission from any tumors. There has been a lot of activity followed by many unknowns and, ultimately, the time of excellent health that I enjoy today.

And this was just one aspect of my life at that time; concurrently, running with so many other parts, projects to complete, and services to provide. Now, this is just one life, and since all life is sacred, multiply this life by so many billions of lives, all connecting, all important, and all filled with powerful events that matter to the individual and to the lives that person touches.

The essential point is this, while all these life-events are important, they are but a tiny portion of a much greater Reality. When you think of the ocean, the waves on the ocean's surface are powerful and produce a lot of activity, still, when compared to what is occurring below the surface, there is so much more ocean below than what is seen on the surface. You soon realize that the surface is but a miniscule percentage of the whole, and while not insignificant, especially to those busy riding the waves, surface living pales in significance to the real power and life found below. Worldly life is the wave action; the great Reality is what lies below.

Papa spent the first thirty-plus years of his life tossed on the waves: as a boy eluding his school teacher to find a quiet spot to read Shakespeare, as a young man learning the textile trade and becoming a husband and father—until he experienced a great awakening that led him in a completely new direction toward his beloved Ram. Mother Hamilton lived as a little girl being hemmed in by the waves: her mother's rules, such as not leaving the yard when playing. She was the object of so much attention because she was the only child of seven to live. Then she became a young woman making her way in the work world while nurturing a glimmer of an awakening thought that there is more to existence and that she has a special destiny. Much lay hidden under the surface until she met her great guru, Paramhansa Yogananda. He opened a window and showed her there was more to life.

For us, what is "below" the surface is experienced, if we are fortunate, in glimpses of a greater Reality—something we know exists but are not very conscious of, even with the glimpses. To get to this greater Reality, we must face a thin film of reality known as the subconscious mind. Through dreams and introspection, we gain a greater awareness of the subconscious mind—those thoughts and emotions that are stored from times past. Sometimes these memories are compressed psychic energy, compressed because they have been repressed. This reservoir of psychic energy can be a powerful player in one's life, making fears and desires create useful and destructive habits that come to us from surprising depths. This psychic energy holds our past; that is, the good, the bad, and the ugly, all ready to bubble up to the surface, potentially costing us an enormous amount of mental energy, especially if we wish to keep it at bay.

Besides the relatively thin layer of the subconscious mind, there is the vast superconscious mind—not usually directly perceived by the conscious mind. When the superconscious mind illumines the conscious mind, it brings inspiration, intuitive flashes of truth, and a higher order of Reality, one that supersedes either the normal waking conscious mind or the oftentimes murky depths of the subconscious mind. Even a glimpse of the beauty and transcendence of the superconscious mind can inspire life to new heights; it awakens our awareness to a new way of experiencing life; it is the doorway to the vast ocean that creates the waves of creation on the surface; and oh, it is so much more.

The superconscious mind reveals what we call God, and God-consciousness. When this awakening occurs, what before may have been dismissed as a myth, because it does not appear to belong to the surface waves of creation of the material world, suddenly takes on more than a theoretical potential; rather, it takes on a living Reality that is undeniable, powerful, and enthralling. The old notion that the world of the five senses, and what the human mind makes of this physical world, is the ultimate reality, falls away, and what is born is a vast Reality, the Reality of the tremendous ocean under the waves.

This under-the-wave Reality is blissful, enlightening, and it leads to the supreme truth. The alternating waves of this material reality fade into a shadowy twilight compared to the rising dawn that reveals a bright and beautiful world all around. The astounded conscious mind discovers this Reality has always been with us, only the ordinary mind simply did not have the light to see it.

The Buddha is a title that means the "Awakened One," having the same meaning as the title The Christ, "The Anointed One." It denotes the one who is awake to this greater Reality—the one who sees it through newly awakened eyes gains a new understanding and develops a new awareness.

All those called to this path are here to awaken to this greater Reality. While we must navigate the waves on the surface of this material reality, nevertheless, our greater task is to explore the immensity below the waves. The story is told of the pearl divers. The pearl divers swim under the surface to find the valuable pearl, but only the divers who are willing to dive deep will discover it and know the wealth it promises. We too must learn to dive deep, to drop further down in meditation, to truly experience the greater Reality. To merely play on the surface will never awaken this deeper life. God is bliss, ever-new joy, shining truth, and a living awareness of the eternal nature of life—all of this awaits the pearl diver who is for God-experience—it awaits you.

May 4

You Shall Be Comforted

Yogacharya David with portrait of Paramhansa Yogananda, 2009.**

Change is the nature of this world. This is a simple fact, yet there is a part of the brain that, to make sense of this world, looks to those predictable things in life to help us to find assurance and order: assurance that the world is safe, order so that we might navigate this world and find happiness. So, while certain parts of the brain are looking for order, change comes and upsets that looked for order—change that can make us feel shaken to the core.

When we enter the spiritual way of seeing things, we seek to transfer our looking for assurance, safety, and order from this world to our growing union with God. But, as Mother affirms: Rome was not built in a day, and neither does anyone attain God-realization overnight. It is a process, certainly, and one we seek to quicken. As Master said: Do not go by the bullock-cart method but take the airplane route. Through deepened God-experience, we recognize that the inner assurance of knowing God is the only constant in life—for everything that is born will die; everything that is created will one day disappear.

Then there are certain things that happen in life that shake us to our core. When Master came to America, he enlisted the help of his friend from India, Swami Dhirananda. Dhirananda came and was a mainstay through the 1920s at Mt. Washington while Master traveled the length and breadth of America giving lectures and classes, nearly non-stop. One day, Dhirananda showed up in New York where Master was lecturing and said he was leaving the organization. He demanded money from Master for the work he had done. Master agreed he needed money to start a new life, and promised payments for years to come. However, the shock of this meeting took the wind out of Master's sails. He even seriously thought of returning to India—permanently. Fortunately for us, he says that the Divine Mother took him by the ear, and told him to continue on. After some time spent in Mexico, he returned to the work God had given him—even though a part of him simply wanted to wander on the banks of the Ganges.

Many "wake-up calls" come to us, challenging our attachment to the way we think this world should be, versus how it is in the moment. It may be illness, death, loss of job, or a relationship; this world can deliver some serious knocks and shocks. In my sadhana, God systematically withdrew from me so many personal landmarks: first, the mahasamadhi of my guru, then the loss of a first marriage, family, home, and profession, taking me through two years of a "Dark Night of the Soul." My sadhana stripped me to the bone, then ground the bones to dust, and then blew the dust to the four corners of the earth. I took a sabbatical from being a minister, stating: "I am empty. How can I serve others when I have nothing, not a thing, I can give?"

What we must know: these "wake-up calls" come with a purpose—to wake us up! The Vedas say: Arise, Awake! When all we have is taken from us, then we must turn to God as our refuge, solace, comforter, and guide. To not do so is to slide into darkness. Even then, much darkness can eventually serve to awaken the Divine within—only, how much suffering occurs between slipping into darkness and doing the hard work of extracting ourselves from the deep well into which we have fallen?

Here is the good news: you may save yourself from depths of despair by going to God now. Turn your attention to Him, in good times and in tough times. If illness creeps up on you, if the pain of sorrow seeks to enfold you in its wings of separateness, if financial misfortunes weigh you down, if relationships betray you—then take God with you. Under stress, we tend to close down. Do the opposite—open up to God. Breathe, open; allow the Divine Current to flow into you; allow the Divine Presence to glow within. Let go of the world, all things of time and space, all outer realities, and focus on God alone.

The Great Master said, "Blessed are they that mourn, for they shall be comforted" (Matthew 5:4). Blessed are they that mourn—the reason you mourn is that you love, and love is the greatest gift of all. Love can be painful when you feel loss, but the Master says you shall be comforted. However, not all who mourn feel comfort. That is because in your loss you feel separated and bereft. But there is a greater truth than isolation, a more profound way of being in this world, and that is remembering that you are forever connected with God, and by turning your mind towards Him, that blessed Spirit comes into you, and you into Him. The Holy Spirit comforts you, assuages the pain, and makes you know that you are never alone.

When Yogananda took the blow, he turned to the Divine Mother for comfort and guidance. And throughout the "Dark Night of the Soul" that God and Guru put me through, I somehow knew that it was Divine Will that was at work. To breathe, open, and allow your Divine Friend, Guide, and Savior to gain entry into your innermost pain and aloneness means that you are on the pathway to wholeness, that you are growing in God—merging into Him even as He is merging into you. The path of the cross, is the path to resurrection—from the pain of separation to the bliss, light, and wisdom of the Perfect One. This is the true assurance that you have so long been looking for—knowing that God is with you always.

May 5

SAINT LYNN

Successful businessman and accomplished yogi,
Rajasi Janakananda, seated in meditation pose.**

On May 5, 1892, James (Jimmy) Lynn, Saint Lynn, as Master referred to him, was born near Archibald, Louisiana. What a remarkable example of a modern businessman becoming an accomplished yogi! For those who say their lives are too busy to meditate, here is a man running multiple business enterprises, a householder with a wife (who was not in favor of his being Master's disciple), managing all the pressures and demands that his position came with, and still, he found time for deep meditation and gained a high spiritual perfection. Master gave Saint Lynn the distinction of the name Rajasi, *king of yogis*.

In a talk given in 1960, Mother recalls Rajasi at a Kriya Initiation:

> I remember that one time Master was giving a *Kriya Initiation* in Los Angeles. When you practice Kriya over a long period of time, you can practice it very little before you go into ecstasy—at a certain time during your development, the Life Force will immediately leave your body. Well, Rajasi was sitting in the front row, and Master was telling all the different devotees how to do Kriya. Rajasi, because he had been doing Kriya for many years was able to leave his body—he was a master in his own right—and he slumped immediately to the floor. Well, Bernard rushed over and pressed the jugular vein in order to bring the Life-force back into the body—yogis have this method where they can return life to the body. So, finally, when Rajasi went in front of Master to receive the initiation, Master laughed at him (and Rajasi had a bald head), and he patted his head, and he said, "Well, you left us for a little while, didn't you?" (Mother laughing)

And this is what Rajasi once said in a talk to devotees:

> One of the blessings I have received in my friendship with Paramhansa Yogananda has been permanent relief from a state of nervousness, a state of strain, an inward state of uncertainty. I have gained calmness, peace, joy, and a sense of security that cannot come to anyone until he has found the true security of the soul. How heavenly is the company of a saint! Of all the things that have come to me in life, I treasure most the blessings that Paramhansaji has bestowed on me.

Rajasi was a tremendous help to Master, both spiritually and materially, and we are the grateful beneficiaries of his taking incarnation with Master so that we might have living examples of what is possible for both human evolution and involution. We bow to the great Light shining through your life, Saint Lynn.

May 12

THE LIFE OF YOGANANDA: MY TAKEAWAY

Paramhansa Yogananda.**

A week after finishing *The Life of Yogananda*, there are some takeaways I have from this biography. The first is how hard Master worked, and the sheer amount he traveled for years while crisscrossing America. Some years, he was at Mt. Washington for merely a few weeks. I know Master said in the *Autobiography* that he loved to travel and see new places, yet this amount of time on the road must have been very challenging. He was here in America to make a difference—and what a difference he made!

The other fact that stands out is how many balls Master was balancing: traveling, speaking, event planning, advertising, and then the classes that followed, responsibility for the Mt. Washington Headquarters, and, with a growing number of churches, and Centers, the financial responsibilities to keep it all going (working to pay off debts much of this time), and fulfilling his role as guru to a growing number of devotees—in person, through letters, and in Spirit.

Then there were the disappointments: those he depended on who did not follow through—even betrayed him, people of wealth saying they would support the work and then giving nothing, having to battle prejudice, people being suspicious of his motives, jealousy, and addressing those who thought that they knew better than he.

And, he rose above these obstacles and challenges; he was a tremendous success. In hindsight, we see his accomplishments; however, hindsight can lose details, and while Master did have support, drew many wonderful souls to him, and is a shining light in this world, it stands out to me what an extraordinary God-man he was to overcome all the trials that God sent to him.

There are those who do not always see the man in the God-man. Some have said that Jesus did not really suffer on the cross, because God could not suffer. Nor could he have had doubts, because how could God doubt? And while it is true that a God-man or a God-woman has access to extraordinary power and consciousness, that one still lives in a human body, faces many of the same trials that any human being does, and can even feel despondent (Rama, an incarnation of God, felt depressed at times when separated from Sita). Acknowledging his humanness only increases our compassion, and appreciation, for all that Master accomplished in his life.

And how may this inform us on our path to God-realization? As Master said, "The same God that is in me, is also in you." We can call upon that same God—the tremendous power, upliftment, and intelligence that made it possible for Master to do all he did—and that Divinity ignites in us the qualities of the all-pow-erful One.

As Mother said of her own condition as a fully realized Being, "I am fully human, and fully Divine." To many, this seems to be an unsolvable paradox, but for the sincere aspirant, it offers inspira-tion—even in our humanness, we are also Divine. Our task is the same that Master and Mother had in their lives—to realize the inner divinity of God. In Master's life, we have a story of just such possibilities, not only for Master or just a chosen few, but for all who aspire.

May 13

MOTHER'S DAY

Yogacharya David and his mother in front of her teacup collection, 2012.

What a perfect idea, to honor mothers everywhere. As Mother Hamilton said, "Every mother goes through pain, and sometimes into the very jaws of death, to bring forth every child which she bears." This was true of my own mother.

God gave me a second experience of being in my mother's womb. I heard my mother's heartbeat; I was so perfectly comfortable being where I was. And, I knew that life on earth would not be an easy one. I felt resistant to leaving that haven of peace in the womb as I listened to that heartbeat. This was such a complete experience that, while going through it, my own physical body was curled up in a fetal position.

I talked with my mother after I had this inner experience about my birth. She said that I was breach (lying sideways in the womb) and that the doctor was up to his elbows, getting me turned. She had tears from this that needed to be sutured, and my aunt Kay came to help her for some weeks after the birth as my mother could not move easily—she had my two older brothers to care for as well as a new baby. Every mother faces the possibility of the unknown and shows great courage in bringing forth new life. When we really think about it, new life is absolutely a miracle, and no new life is possible without a mother.

Today, we salute our mothers. I feel great gratitude, not only for my own mother, but all mothers; they made a decision to create life, and life is a miracle.

Since I not only have a physical mother, without whom I would not have this incarnation, I also have my spiritual Mother, without whom I would not have a life worth living. Plato compared himself to a midwife, helping to bring forward a new being, a spiritually-born individual. A guru takes it further. The guru delivers spiritual shakti or the power of the Divine Mother, thereby playing an essential part, ensuring that the Christ, or Krishna, child takes birth in the aspirant. Then, the guru shepherds the soul through all the experiences the soul must go through in order to know God.

Babaji described how he watched over the soul of Lahiri Mahasaya: when he left the body in a previous incarnation, moved with him in Spirit as he spent a lifetime in the astral, then kept him under a protective wing when he was just a little tyke, and until he grew into manhood. How loving Babaji was with his beloved disciple—watching, protecting, and secretly guiding him until it was ordained that they should meet again in the physical.

Mother Hamilton, willing to expend herself completely, entered the "jaws of death" to help bring about the total restoration of

God-consciousness to all whom God had given her. I know that even when we are not aware, she watches over us, helps us to overcome our karma, and know the Infinite. Motherhood requires patience: from the zygote, fetus, newborn, to a graceless teen, and all the in-between stages, we will not appear like a finished product, not at all. Yet, the guru never ceases to see the perfect soul in God that each one of us truly is. Oh, such patience, what forbearance, that only God-consciousness can display!

I bow to you, my blessed Divine Mother. May your Grace lift us up and guide us through the great transformation; may we merge into God, and God into us. Inspire us to be what we should be in God, and help us know the perfect freedom of Spirit—to be immersed in the bliss you experience, and in the supreme wisdom that you know.

To all who are Mothers, have a blessed Mother's Day.

Mother to us all: Mother Hamilton, 1981.

May 20

KALI: THE FIERCE FACE OF GOD

Kali: The fierce face of the
Divine Mother, Dakshineswar
Kali Temple, Calcutta, India.

This last Sunday, I spoke about Kali—the fierce image of the Divine Mother. As usual, when I experience God speaking through me, I am also being taught. In my uplifted state during the talk, God showed me a deeper meaning behind the imagery of Kali. For, in all sacred images and stories, there are greater truths being alluded to—sacred imagery is always pointing to the supreme Reality. However, when the story is taken only at its face value, the mind becomes fixated on the fascinating but bewildering outer images of the parable. Jesus said, "Therefore speak I to them in parables: because they, seeing, see not; and hearing, they hear not, neither do they understand" (Matthew 13:13). "For this people's heart is waxed gross, and their ears are dull of hearing, and their eyes they have closed" (Matthew 13:15), but "Blessed are your eyes, for they see; and your ears, for they hear" (Matthew 13:16).

For those who focus on the outer story alone, debates ensue, and the reasoning mind can easily pick apart such images and tales for their inconsistencies, historical inaccuracies, and sometimes, just plain illogic. Predictions of a future savior can fit into this category. For the past three thousand years, there has been the prediction of a Messiah (Mashiach) in Judaism—a righteous king, such as David, who brings peace to this world and ends hunger. Christians have been waiting two thousand years for the second coming, for Christ to appear from the clouds of heaven, and bring a thousand years of peace. And for the past 1,400 years, many Muslims have waited in anticipation for the return of the 12th Imam to bring peace and justice to this world. Coincidently, the looked-for return of these saviors will usher in the supremacy of their respective religions——leaving only one religion standing. Since these three literal scenarios are mutually exclusive, only one of them can be correct. Of course, none think their own religion will be on the losing side but see themselves standing triumphant over their stunned competitors.

Now, you can either be a believer in one of these looked-for prophecies or see the whole thing as hopeless confusion, or perhaps use these histories to analyze current-day events. (Today, many orthodox Christians are in support of making Jerusalem the official seat of government for Israel because predictions in the Bible state that this is a prelude to the return of the Christ.) However, for the practical spiritual aspirant, the understanding comes that, from the beginning, these predictions were not intended to be worldly-based. Rather, the savior parable is a description of a coming inner, spiritual, illumination, for the striving devotee. New Jerusalem is a name for an enlightened state of consciousness—and the predicted thousand years of peace is the same as the thousand petalled lotus—the spiritually illumined brain.

For those who perceive the one true Creator behind all religious impulses the world over, then, as Mother Hamilton stated, there is only one God and one religion—a religion beyond secular divisions. There is only one supreme truth—and all the various religions are but descriptions of our human relationship with that truth, or God. In the end, all religions are expressions are the same human desire to know God.

For God to be true, then, the Divine Principle upon which God is understood, must be universal—equally true, for all. Mathematics is true no matter what language you speak, or where you are from; even if you are from another planet, the principles of math will be the same. The symbols that we call numbers can look different, depending on your native land; language may differ, but the unfolding logic of math must be the same. Similarly, the logic for realizing God, and the experience of knowing God, will follow certain universal principles, no matter your language, culture, customs, or religion.

To truly appreciate a religion, you must unlock its symbols—other religions can look alien simply because the language and symbols are not familiar to you. In India, Mother Kali is a much-worshipped form of the Divine Mother. On the surface, one may wonder why? So many images of God are pleasing, but she is not. That fierce image of Kali is intentional and filled with meaning. We may explore its meaning when we break through the cocoon of the outer story and take wing on the direct perception of truth.

As God was showing me while I was giving the talk, the fierce face of Kali, with her accompanying symbols, is the outer form only—the outer fierceness symbolizes this world. Just as the image of Kali is terrible, tongue dripping blood, holding a sword, skulls hanging about, so too can this world be terrifying with wars, famines, pestilence, illness, and suffering of so many varieties. Yet, mystics from time immemorial tell us that the world is God. The world is a sacred expression of its Creator. One can wonder how anyone can say that when there is so much hardship? It is because the mystic dives deeper and comes up with a magnificent pearl of wisdom. The spiritual master sees not merely the outer fierceness of the world but perceives the Divine Presence underlying all creation. To the penetrating mind, the beautiful Divine Mother reveals Herself behind the ugly image of Kali and the suffering of the world.

That guiding Kali-Presence ensures that the suffering engendered by the horrors of this world eventually leads aspirants to the truth of detachment. Detachment is necessary for Self-realization. With realization comes true freedom beyond the thralldom of this world—for true freedom is oneness with God.

Our shortcut to knowing this freedom is to acknowledge that the things of this world can never bring lasting happiness. We do not need to wait for the harshness of this world to tear us from our clinging to the body and things of the world, for the alternating currents of good and evil will ever be a part of our experience in this life. To practice detachment from duality, and to put our minds on God, is the pathway to mystical union with the Infinite. Seen from this perspective, the fierce face of God wakes the soul from its indifference; it challenges the narrative of worldly attachments and sets us on our way to realizing the sacred Divine Presence. Then, through eyes informed by the Divine Presence, the beauty of the Creator is seen shining throughout all creation.

I, once, had a beautiful demonstration of grace through the Divine Mother as Kali. In pilgrimage, I was at the temple of Dakshineswar, in India. It was here that the great Ramakrishna worshiped the image of Kali, and where he came to realize God. While walking the temple complex, I came to the Kali Temple just as the doors were opened to reveal the statue of Kali. There was a large crowd pressing in to see the image. As I stood behind the crowd, I thought that while I did want to see the statue that Ramakrishna had worshipped, I did not want to enter this press of humanity.

As I stood apart from all the people, with Swami Vishwananda beside me, a side door of the temple opened; a priest came out and walked directly over to me. He took my hand and indicated that I should come with him—I followed him back to the side door. Swami Vishwananda came in behind me, and we were ushered through an inner hallway right up front to the image of Kali; the pressing crowd was behind us, separated by a gate. The temple priest did not say a word, but gracefully arranged for this darshan of the Mother Kali in such a remarkable way. Why I was singled out is a mystery; one can only say the Divine Mother wished it so.

Just as the Divine Mother arranged for this darshan, so God arranges for knowing the Divine Presence for the sincere and aspiring heart, bypasses the fierce noisiness and confusion of this world, and takes us into our inner temple of silence where the Divine Mother reveals Herself. The message comes: we should not be dissuaded by the outer fierceness of the image of Kali, or of this sometimes-harsh world, but we should dive deep into devotional meditation to find the pearl of realization that reveals the beauty of God, both within and without.

May 27

STILLNESS IS REAL SILENCE

Yogacharya David on the deck of his
retreat cabin at Cloud Mountain, 2000.

Rebecca has come here to stay for some of the last days of her month-long silence and seclusion. Her time for doing this sadhana reminds me of my spending one year in silence and seclusion at Cloud Mountain. This came about when one day I was speaking to a devotee and out of my mouth came, "I feel directed to spend one year in silence." This pronouncement came as the biggest surprise to me—particularly since, previous to this,

I had not spent even one day in meditational silence. But now that God had said it, how would I go about doing it?

I thought of renting a cabin for the year, and others pointed out different silent retreat centers to contact, and one thing led to another (which is another way of saying that God was leading me by the hand, step by step) and I discovered David Branscom and the Cloud Mountain Retreat Center in Southwest Washington. I talked with David, who had started out his spiritual life feeling deeply connected to Master. He had built Cloud Mountain with his own hands, literally carrying the lumber and all materials on his back from the road he had made to the building sites. Although it was mostly Vipassana Buddhists who rented his retreat center at that time, he was thrilled to have someone connected with Master staying at his unique and newly built cabin for a long-term retreatant. He offered the cabin and food for one year at no fee, but I felt I should pay him something. I think we settled on $250 a month. He was lovingly supportive all through the year. I cannot thank him enough for his open-hearted seva.

I knew going in, starting September of the year 2000, it would take some time to settle into silence—particularly since I had been traveling non-stop to Centers, giving talks, and meeting with aspirants. During the first three weeks or so in silence, I could feel my whole being gradually becoming quieter. One of the first things I noted was the absence of movement—being at the cabin, and on the grounds of the five-acre retreat center only—whereas before there were simple and familiar activities, like going to the store, being out and about, and now, nothing. And then there was the absence of planning: no schedules to keep, no arrangements needed tending. My task was silence: be here, be now. I was simply observing, noticing these changes, as time unfolded. And then there was the blessed relief I experienced; there was nowhere to go, nothing to plan, no outward demands—oh the luxury of just being with God!

There were many internal journeys through the year, great challenges, and tremendous experiences given by God and Gurus, experiences that amazed and deeply moved me. However, beyond all of these many wonderful revelations, the real purpose for the year of silence and seclusion came clear to me sometime later in my time there and then continued afterward. I was to be established in the Presence of God.

Twenty-four years prior, Mother had ignited the kundalini force at the base of my spine that then shot like a rocket to the ajna. This was the real beginning of my inward sadhana. There are things we do in our outer sadhana, such as developing the habit of meditation, practicing Kriya Yoga, chanting, and deepening prayer: methods we adopt in order to purify the body and mind. Inner sadhana occurs, with God and Gurus' blessings, when we experience the upward current of the vastly powerful spiritual force, which, in India, is called the kundalini. I could never relate all the experiences I have had with this miraculous kundalini force. It was through these experiences that the inner change occurred; it involved not only Spirit but mind and body, as well. If I had been a better devotee, I am sure I could have shortened the time of transformation. However, through the years, transformation did occur, and it prepared me for merging into Higher Consciousness—the goal of mystics and saints the world over.

God had led me into silence and seclusion, and as a result of what He did, there was a solidification in my oneness with the inner Divine Presence. A strong point of this connecting union was in the Heart Center. I was deeply aware of this steadfast, unchanging, Presence that was unshakable and unvarying. This place of oneness was such that it did not deviate, even when I reentered the world after the year of seclusion. This knowing oneness with the Infinite was a product of God and Gurus' Grace, and with the invaluable help of my "second spiritual Mother," dearest Swami Satchidananda.

When God commanded this year in silence and solitude, I had no idea of what was in store; I only knew it was by His command. Every devotee has his or her own journey, and as we know, paths to God vary in outward form. However, for most, there will come a time of stepping away from the demands of the world to be absorbed into inner silence.

Not speaking is not the real silence (it is amazing how loud and nonstop the mind can be!). Only by stilling the body and mind do we beget true stillness. Then, inner stillness is born in the heart: a place of deep connection with the Infinite Divine that is the firm foundation for oneness with God. To become still is the goal of Kriya Yoga and its after-effect. The chanting of God's name is meant to result in that same stillness. To be established in inner stillness brings about the extraordinary state of oneness. That is why the great mystic sage King David sang, "Be still, and know that I am God" (Psalms 46:10). Be still, and know God as the eternal Self of our Being, the Source of unending bliss, and the answer to all of our heart's desires.

May 28

Honoring Memorial Day

The tent became a house: Elmer is Yogacharya David's grandfather.

After the Civil War, it became a tradition to decorate the graves of soldiers killed in battle. With over 600,000 dead soldiers from that terrible war, there were very few families not touched by the tremendous toll. With time, the honoring of those who gave their lives in battle continued with World War I and II and with subsequent actions by the military. The end of May continues to be a time of honoring and remembering.

For many, the day is also a time for remembering family members who are no longer here. My father took a leading role in organizing flowers for the graves of family members buried in the Yakima Valley. Since childhood, and down to recent years,

Memorial Day was an annual family gathering. My parents, aunts, and assorted relatives made processions to graveyards in Sunnyside and Zillah to place potted plants on or near grave-stones. And we were joined by thousands of others who also gathered at their own family gravesites to do the same. With a large Hispanic population in the area, the tradition is very festive; there are bright, shiny decorations, large pictures of more-recently passed relatives, and many sit in lawn chairs making a day of it. For all, the graveyards bring a quiet reflection, are well attended, and are vibrant with color in honor of the passed soldiers, ancestors, and family members.

It is a day for telling stories about family members. My aunt Kay, in particular, was a keen family historian, recounting memories and family lore. This was always a favorite part of the tradition. One such story was about my great-grandfather and mother. Aaron came to the Yakima Valley as a young man with many dreams. He purchased desert land cheaply, traded a pig for some sapling fruit trees, and he built a house—well, really, it was a tent. It would be some time the next year before the canal was to be built, so he made a yoke, hung a bucket on each end, and would set off to the river, a few miles away, to fetch water for drinking, bathing, and watering his fruit trees.

As a young man, he thought prospects were looking good—it was a good time to marry. However, the sage-covered desert did not bloom young ladies at the time, so he set off over the mountain pass to the big city of Tacoma. There, he met a young woman who had moved with her family from Nova Scotia. Now Tacoma and Nova Scotia share the fact they are near water, and both have green trees and vegetation. They met, decided to marry, and Nellie moved with her new husband to their new "home" in the desert. It was January, and it was cold and bleak. Apparently, either he had oversold the state of his "home" (that is the general consensus among the ladies of the family) or she had imagined it to be more than it was, but she was definitely not happy with the state of things as she found them. A cold dreary January, a few sticks in the desert ground that would someday be an orchard, and a tent to live in were not what she had anticipated!

However, these pioneers were made of tough stock. "You do what you have to do" to get by, survive, and work for a better future. They, as a couple, had a deep faith in God, and eventually built their wood-framed and clad home. It had a proper roof and sporting glazed windows—the house continues to stand on the same property today. It is now surrounded by shade trees and orchards with other farms stretching off across a verdant valley. What changes water and hard work can bring to a desert when the ground is anciently fertilized by rich volcanic ash from nearby Mount Rainier and Adams. Like many in America, the dream has been that you can work hard and build a future—not just for yourself, but for prospective generations as well.

Memorial Day is also called Decoration Day, for decorating the graves with flowers, and for giving homage to those who went before us. As we grow in spiritual awareness, gratitude is something that grows as well. None of us would be here if not for our ancestors. We would not have the life we have if there had not been those willing to give their lives for a greater cause. We have much to be grateful for, and though today we may not live close to those festively-clad graveyards, we can decorate the memories of those who have gone before us with flowering gratitude.

I bow in gratitude to my ancestors, to all our ancestors, and affirm that with our hard work, we may pass down better lives to future generations, and that the day will come when wars and terrorism are but memories, and the only "trumpet calls" we hear are the ones that awaken our souls to God.

June 3

GUIDING INTELLIGENCE

"Consider the lilies of the field" (Matthew 6:28).**

O ccasionally, I hear the arguments from atheists, "There is no proof of God." And yet, a glance around us demonstrates an intelligence so monumental as to convince any open skeptic. The idea that the universe, the earth, and the biosphere of the earth could all happen by random mutations and chance, even allowing for billions of years of evolution, really cannot explain the complexity of design that goes into a flower, an animal, or a human being.

The human body is demonstration enough. In the human body, there are a hundred trillion cells (estimates vary, 37 to 100 trillion). Imagine that, a hundred trillion cells: ten times that of many micro-organisms (good bacteria), operating in the gut (some call this the "forgotten" organ); cells working in an efficient manner, keeping the heart pumping, and many other organs all performing uncountable functions each moment. Could a human intelligence design and make such a body? While we are busy mapping the body and describing many of its functions, we are light years, if ever, away from being able to make a fully human body from scratch. And yet, that is what this universe has done.

And the human body is just a fragment of all creation—the atomic and sub-atomic functions that sustain and surround us, the unmeasured stellar systems—look in any direction, see miraculous life, self-creating, refining, and improving. It is quite a lot to take in. And yet, in its colossal nature, this physical creation is but God's footstool (Isaiah 66:1).

And, for all the magnificence of this creation we see all around us, it is merely reflected intelligence. When we look at a building, we see the reflected intelligence of the architect, not the intelligence itself, of the man or woman who designed the building. If we want to know that intelligence itself, it would help to have a conversation with the architect, and we would then understand the nature of his or her thought about what went into the design and the construction—there is so much to be learned. Add another layer, and see if you can actually experience his or her mind at work—get a glimpse into his or her inner intelligence. For example, experience his or her thoughts in your own mind.

More, now consider once again the creative intelligence that has gone into bringing forth life, all of life—imagine being able to get a glimpse of that mind! Albert Einstein, the great physicist, famously said, "I want to know God's thoughts—the rest are mere details." What a wonderful concept. And this is what mystics and yogis proclaim: still the human mind and be illumined with the way of knowing things, even as God does.

This is quite a statement; yet, what if we could see this world as God sees it? When Jesus picked up a simple lily flower and said, "Consider the lilies how they grow: they toil not, they spin not; and yet I say unto you, that Solomon in all his glory was not arrayed like one of these" (Luke 12:27). What was Jesus seeing in that lily? Was he seeing it as God sees it? I think, "Yes."

I have seen this world transform into a living expression of Divinity. I think, "Yes, this is how God sees creation—perfect, blissful, and an expression of purity and beauty." And then we look out, and we fail to see the world with those qualities? Perhaps it is because we do not see this world as God sees it. Perhaps we insist on our own interpretation of what we see. Perhaps we are insisting on our own ignorance—our own limited vision of what truly is. Indeed, as Jesus said in the Gospel of St. Thomas, "The kingdom of heaven is spread upon the earth, but men do not see it." It is time to know the mind of God, to awaken to an entirely new way of seeing this world.

June 7

I Stand at a Crux in My Life

Yogacharya David at the Basilica of Saint Elizabeth
Ann Seton, Emmitsburg, Maryland, 2017.**

stand at a crux in my life. In fact, the reality of each and every moment is a crux—a crucial space in time that holds infinite possibilities. It is only a habit of mind that makes us focus on a narrow spectrum of reality, that makes us think that we and our world are not touched by a transcendent beauty, power, and intelligence. By making conscious contact with infinite Reality, we open access to so much more than what we ordinarily think of as self. By claiming this higher Reality as our own, we become new, whole.

There are many science fiction stories about time travel, about going to alternate universes and realities—they can have interesting scenarios with twists and turns, but what remains unchanged is the personality of the individual, the perception of self. That is why simply changing the outer circumstance of life may give a temporary lift or a hit, but it does not create the real change that, deep down, we are looking for.

Similarly, the fantasy of being wealthy, famous, and adored by others, may seem to promise happiness, but we need only look to the tabloids to see that these attainments do not guarantee fulfillment. As a comedian once said, "I know that money cannot buy happiness, but I would just like to have enough to prove it."

God once showed me a previous life in which I had been the governor of an enormous province and lived much like a king. But, even with wealth and total power, I was lonely and unfulfilled. This experience helped to teach me that real happiness cannot be bought. I, like so many of us, have been programmed to believe in the worldly dream of success. It may take many such lifetimes to convince us otherwise, but eventually, we come to understand that this world simply cannot satisfy us in the long run.

This realization can bring us to a crisis point; if the world cannot do it, and we cannot imagine anything greater than this world, then why exist? And some will take their lives, but that does not work either, because we find ourselves right back in a body, facing that questioning moment all over again. At last, that emptiness, loneliness, and yearning for something greater, leads us to long for that "something more" above this horizontal plane of material existence. This need now takes us further than simply to an idea that there must be a heaven waiting for us at the end of life, for at this point, we cannot wait and defer for some hoped-for future happiness. The yearning is here and now: we must know the truth.

It is at this moment of realization that we really enter the path to realization. Note these famous words that relate to this stage of our journey, words said after the British defeated Rommel at Alamein in North Africa:

> This is not the end, this is not even the beginning of the end, this is just perhaps the end of the beginning.
> —WINSTON CHURCHILL

The clearer we are that this world does not contain what our heart longs for, then the more rapidly we progress on the path. We then continuously remember that while we live, and participate in this world, our minds are ever turned toward the transcendent One, each and every moment.

When, through deepened meditation, and a purified consciousness, we touch the fabric of God, we open to an infinite field of possibilities. Outwardly, our life may look much the same; inwardly, we are transformed. We now know that the Lord of the universe resides in our heart; a fountain of bliss is ever playing through our spine and brain; universal love flows through our heart; and wisdom-thoughts illumine our mind—in short, we have all that our heart truly ever longed for. This makes each moment a crux in our life because through our divine contact, all possibilities reside in us—there can be nothing ordinary or humdrum in our life ever again.

June 10

THE CRISIS

Thomas Paine, portrait by Auguste Millere, c. 1876.**

My country is the world, and my religion is to do good.
—THOMAS PAINE

Upon waking this morning, thoughts streamed in from the superconscious mind that included the phrase, "These are the times that try men's souls." Then, following that stream of thought: "There are times in life when great trials come; other times, when life has a happier nature; and these two alternating experiences can be graphed like a sine wave, or a financial chart of rolling stock, as they move up and down—an inevitable movement in life."

It was Thomas Paine who wrote words about trying times, entitled *The Crisis*. It was toward the beginning of the American Revolution when a small number of militia, farmers, and silver smiths untrained in war, took up arms against what at that time was the greatest army and navy in the world—and things were not going well. Not only do such crises occur in fields of military action, but in family life, professional life, and very importantly, in our spiritual pursuit. From the first paragraph of Paine's inspired writing, we may borrow its wisdom and strength to meet our own crisis when it comes.

> THESE are the times that try men's souls. The summer soldier and the sunshine patriot will, in this crisis, shrink from the service of their country; but he that stands by it now, deserves the love and thanks of man and woman. Tyranny, like hell, is not easily conquered; yet we have this consolation with us, that the harder the conflict, the more glorious the triumph. What we obtain too cheap, we esteem too lightly: it is dearness only that gives everything its value. Heaven knows how to put a proper price upon its goods; and it would be strange indeed if so celestial an article as FREEDOM should not be highly rated.[19]

Is it not true, "What we obtain too cheap, we esteem too lightly?" My thoughts were then guided to Mother Hamilton and the life she lived, enduring one trial and difficulty after another. It was destined that she would chart a new course largely on her own, unaided by an organization, and often not understood by

---

19   Thomas Paine. https://www.ushistory.org

those around her. Yet, her determination, the will of steel under her velvet-love for God, Guru, and humanity, never wavered.

We can draw so many lessons of loyalty and strength of resolve from Mother's life. Life can challenge us to the core, and if the goal is high (And what is higher than God-realization?), then the price must be steep. To paraphrase Krishna in the Gita:

> Fight the good fight with all your strength and be ever focused on God. Whether you win or lose in the outer sense is not in your control, that is up to Me (God). But whether you win or lose, by staying focused on Me, you win the spiritual battle by being aligned with truth and ever advancing in Self-realization.

Tyranny, like hell, is not easily conquered; yet we have this consolation with us, that the harder the conflict, the more glorious the triumph. When you conquer hell by realizing God, the glory of triumph is not a ticker tape parade, or your picture in the paper, but it is the bliss that wells up from deep within; it is the Light of your eternal Being blazing, and it is the revelation of inspired wisdom from the Infinite.

Anchor yourself in this thought in times of crisis, and in times of ease: God, Gurus, and all the saints and spiritual masters who have ever tread this path of realization are with me. Awareness of the fact that I never stand alone means that when I touch the fabric of God's Being through remembrance of Him, I touch the glory of all that He is!

June 14

THE ONE INDISPENSABLE THING

Yogacharya David, Spokane River, Washington, 2016.**

God has me working more in the world lately as we are doing some remodeling on this house. Planning, arranging, and following up with contractors, making sure everything is ready, and that they have what they need—He has me fully enabled and fully engaged. There is a wonderful feeling to have the switch turned on, allowing me to participate in this world. I always enjoy working in this world as I have done since an early age, up to the time when He drew me more inwardly to Himself.

As spiritual aspirants, the crux of living in this world is for us to fully participate in it, and not be separated from our true Self as a result. Events can come in rapid fire; for example, demands to make decisions, to make the body and mind function even when they are resistant to doing so, with success bringing its own challenges, tempting you to think that you are the doer. So, in challenging times, or during smooth sailing, these worldly occupations make it a necessity to have a highly focused sadhana-practice.

A devotee wrote to me: "Things will go along, and I'll make one decision to do something, and then things are all out of whack. My decisions are often not made from the heart, because of this or that. Things just seem to come at me so fast. I cannot even stop to connect to the light before making a decision." To one degree or another, isn't this a dilemma for each of us while we are living in this world?

The key to maintaining our balance is the intensity of our practice—it has to meet or exceed the intensity of worldly demands. Now someone (not you of course) may say, "I have barely enough energy to keep things going in this world as it is, never mind adding another thing to my plate, like having to remember God!" And if we think of it as only another task on our to-do list, added to those things we are already not getting done, then that might be right.

However, God-remembrance is not simply another task—it is our primary task. Not only that, but just as importantly, staying connected with God—our real Self—brings important benefits that will actually help us in our worldly life. These benefits are the real secret in life so that we can have both a full and a fulfilling life.

The first benefit is that in God-awareness, we remain in a calm center. Like a skilled athlete, we operate in "the zone" where there is a natural flow in body and mind. From that calm center, we are in a prime position to use the reasoning mind as well as the intuitional mind. Like a general observing the field of combat, we see the movement of forces and calculate what needs to be done, not overwhelmed by the noise and confusion of war. This calm reason adds and subtracts based on experience and learning. The intuitional mind does not add or subtract, at least not consciously—it knows through direct perception what is true. Intuition comes, not through reasoning, but as a flash of insight. Both reason and intuition are required to ensure successful functioning in this world.

Being Self-centered means that we adhere to the highest standards. Abiding by right action, according to our reason, helps purify our mind, which will then give us access to truth from intuition. Through intuition, we know what is true, not only for ourselves, but for others as well. Honing this skill, of knowing what is right action, saves us from disastrous mistakes. Right action, or dharma, is the most efficient means forward, both in this world and spiritually. While wrong action can look more expedient in the moment, it inevitably builds resistant karma that immediately, or eventually, causes suffering, and undermines our success.

Our spiritual practice bears the fruit of bliss, light, and universal love on our tree of consciousness. All of humanity seeks happiness, but so many seek it in this world only. A deeper analysis reveals that this world can never yield the kind of happiness we truly seek. Some will say our "reward" comes in an afterlife—do not seek it here. Mystics and yogis have asserted that we have access to that "reward" right here, and right now, but not through worldly means. Spiritual happiness is bliss, is to be found within, and in the present—and while it is latent in most, nevertheless, it is available to all.

Having our happiness already in place enables us to give perfect service to this world. With our happiness in place, it is easy to detach from outcomes. It is our internal joy that now fuels our participation in life, not some hoped-for outcome or fantasy afterlife. Of course, we have goals for what to do, and what we want to have as a result, but our happiness is not dependent on such outward rewards. As a result, we are centered in our Self, not identified with the things of the world. This detachment gives us a balance and a perspective that makes us more proficient in our activities.

And the price of entry for discovering this here-and-now reward of spiritual attributes? It is, of course, to keep our mind on God: to breathe, to be a mindful witness of all experiences, to keep our attention at the ajna (the point between the eyebrows), to chant His name, and to meditate deeply upon Him. Love is the most powerful attractor in this world and beyond. Love of God automatically brings about detachment. Love of God is the most powerful asset for living in the world, but not being of it.

Let us practice, practice, practice until we are living in the "spiritual zone" and feeling God's joyful Presence within us, until we are centered in our deeper Self, no matter our outer circumstances, and until our inborn dharma spontaneously guides us to right action. By enacting this practice, we receive life-giving energy (supplying us with far more than we give in our practice). It is not simply another task to add to our "to-do list," it is the one indispensable thing to do when fulfilling daily duties in this world while serving our Infinite Beloved.

June 17

IN GRATITUDE TO FATHERS

The loving compassionate Father. *God the Father*, painting
by Giovanni Battista Cima de Conegliano, c. 1510–1517.

Today, we celebrate fathers for the vital role they play in the
human drama of family. Indeed, when fathers are absent,
families and communities suffer, so fathers are an essential
part of both family and community.

One of the great changes that has occurred in the past twenty
or thirty years is the positive involvement of fathers in raising
children. Many in my father's generation, and generations before,
observed role distinctions where mothers raised the children
and fathers provided for, and protected, the family. Machines,

technology, and changing role definitions, have freed fathers to have the time and energy to devote to family. The trend toward a more involved father has been a huge shift, one in which the father is more intimately connected with his children—this is win-win for the father and his children.

There was a woman sociologist who looked at the voluntary role a father plays for his family, in comparison to living only for himself. To financially provide for himself only would require far less effort on his part, without the need for a family home, food, clothes, and education for his children. Her point was that the father puts forward a tremendous effort to provide for his family, often without much acknowledgment—it is done quietly, expectedly, and without much fanfare. How grateful we are for those fathers who make sacrifices for family, often playing an invisible, but a most essential, role for those they love.

In many of the great Western traditions, the father archetype came to symbolize God, or the chief god, such as Zeus. With the great master, Jesus, we get the most touching, intimate, connection with Father as God, or Abba, in Jesus' Aramaic. Now, to some, it may sound heretical to give God a gender, but the truth is that metaphors are powerful symbols used to bring out certain positive qualities in us. Clearly, for Jesus, Father was an endearing term for God that touched his heart, made him feel close and intimate with the Divine Presence, a presence that existed both in his own soul, and as the creative power and intelligence that manifest as this entire universe. Far from the fiery, rule-making God of Moses, Jesus' Father is loving, understanding, and giving—He doesn't even mind a little rule-breaking if it preserves the spirit of the law!

So, today, I give honor to my father and grandfathers, and our beloved Father in Heaven. To my father and grandfathers, I feel such gratitude for all your hard work that conveyed your love for family far more eloquently than you ever expressed in words. And, for my Father in Heaven, may we all feel the same intimacy that Jesus felt in relationship with You—such love, care, and closeness. And for all of you fathers today, who work and strive to make your families safe, secure, and loved, I give you thanks.

June 21

THE SALUBRIOUS SUMMER SOLSTICE

Sri Yukteswarji and Master Yogananda at a Summer Solstice
Celebration, at Sri Yukteswar's Hermitage, Serampore, India, 1935.

The summer solstice is upon us, and we feel the powerful vibrations of this hallmark event. Sri Yukteswarji made this an event each year, with chanting, feasting, and a talk he gave under the stars. What a lovely picture that makes in our minds as we think of sitting at the Master's feet, absorbing the vibrant atmosphere of this spiritually charged occasion.

It is a fascinating idea that we are so strongly connected with all of creation, such that distant constellations of stars could be influencing us here on earth. We all certainly feel the effects of lunar cycles. We all know that there are mysterious rhythms in our lives in which things either go uncommonly smoothly or, it seems that we are fighting invisible currents of opposition all the way.

The warp and woof of these events can be chalked up to chance, but isn't it possible that there are lawfully-governed undercurrents in life that we can sometimes trace, even anticipate?

In our perception of these outer influences, it is important to know that we have a power deep within that supersedes all outer influences. Whether we come into contact with a negative personality, situation, or contrary stellar influence, we are reminded that the power of God within is greater. This does not mean that we will not have to contend with outer forces, but that we should not give them preeminence in our mind. The light, intelligence, love, and joy of God are superior to creation, and tapping into that internal power is our best weapon for combating negative influences.

Of course, these outer influences are not only negative—there are powerful external forces that help lift us up as well. The proximity of highly developed souls in our life, salubrious situations that support our spiritual aspirations, and the turning of the celestial clock at such times as the Summer Solstice, all can bring the positive. Sri Yukteswarji tells us that this is a special time. By spreading our meditational wings, we can benefit from the powerful upward drafts that are present at this time.

Let us join together in Spirit and feel the rising currents—the power and bliss of our Infinite Beloved. Let Sri Yukteswarji's blessings shower Grace upon us all, renewing our world during this longest day, the Summer Solstice.

June 24

INTO THE STILLNESS

Sri Yukteswarji: Master of Stillness, c. 1913.

Stillness is one of the great virtues of spiritual consciousness. Some might associate stillness with death: a dead body
does not breathe, move, or show signs of life. A yogi, one
in union with God, may not breathe, (or breathe very shallowly),
may not show signs of life, yet such stillness is the opposite of
death—dead, perhaps to the world for a while, but by no means
is there the inertness of a dead body.

The inner stillness of the yogi comes with deepened meditation; the body becomes quiet, and the mind enters into the great
stillness—awareness continues, but the constant monologue of

the mind stops. When I have been out cross-country skiing or snow-shoeing, the swish or crunch of snow is all that makes noise. Suddenly, coming to a stop, the snowflakes quietly fall, and there is total quiet, such a hush is all around—a remarkable feeling. There is an element of that hush in this inner stillness, a feeling of magic, almost, of awe, that moves the soul.

But such stillness does not come easily to a culture that is all about movement, doing things, and constant stimulation of the senses. When I was in silence and seclusion for a year, we had a couple of retreat weekends in which devotees joined me in silence. However, there was much note-writing at times, giggling, and laughing. One person continued to talk in a whisper (some-how thinking that was keeping silence!) while saying: "I would like to be in a silent retreat for a prolonged time." Real silence is not so easy.

However, with deepened practice, we can touch that realm of inner silence that gives us true rest. We practice our kriya, chant God's name, meditate on Hong Sau, and suddenly we find our-selves dropping into that inner realm of stillness—even if for just a moment. On headstones of the dead, we read, "Rest in peace," and can imagine, "Oh, that one is finally getting true rest from living life on this earth." The truth is, we can have that rest even while in the body when the restless tides of the breath are finally stilled. It may be a challenge, but what a worthwhile challenge!

To begin, let us use our imagination. It is most common, when attempting to enter silence, that we are aware of how un-silent we are! Let us use our mind's ability to conjure images: of being in the quiet of a snowy paradise, or entering into the precincts of an ancient temple and sitting at the feet of a venerable saint—let our mind rest in those peaceful surroundings, being fully aware, but very still. Let that quiet saturate our soul and nurture us in peace. Simply reside there—no place to go, nothing to do, just be in the stillness.

As we learn to attune our mind to this stillness, we find that we can carry it into our daily life. It may be easiest while we are walking in the woods, or by a body of water, or while tending our garden. However, with practice, we can also experience this inner stillness while meeting with others or doing ordinary tasks throughout the day. Just imagine being in that quiet stillness all through the day. How would we then feel at the end of the day? Would there be less stress in our body? Would we have more energy? And notice, do we feel good about decisions made from that place of stillness?

Learn to touch upon the power of stillness; make it a part of a daily practice. David spoke a great truth when he said, "Be still, and know that I AM God" (Psalm 46:10). True stillness takes us beyond ourselves; stillness is the gateway to realizing our oneness with the Infinite. Sri Yukteswarji wrote in *The Holy Science* that knowing God fulfills all of our heart's desires. That being the case, when we enter into the silence of God-consciousness, we are perfectly content, and this awareness loops back into even greater stillness—we no longer have need of our constant, restless, nature, and it simply drops away. So, let us begin, now.

June 28

TWO YEARS FREE AND CLEAR

Yogacharya David in the desert,
Badlands National Park, South Dakota.**

ealth Report: Dr. S., my saintly surgeon confirmed that all
is well. Blood tests, PET scan, CT scan, and MRI—the best
diagnostic tools modern medicine has to offer—confirm
that I am tumor free and that my overall health is excellent. It
has been two years now since I had a liver resection to remove a
tumor, and two and a half years since I had tumors removed from

my small intestines. These operations saved the life of this body, and there has been no sign of tumors since.

While the health of the body is not the absolute arbiter of fulfillment, it certainly is an important ingredient to our abilities and our pleasures in day-to-day activities. A malfunctioning body, and accompanying physical pain, can dominate the mind, and affect our mood. To a greater or lesser degree, sensations from the body, and our ability to move and breathe, will make demands on our attention. However, to be master of ourselves, we must be the gatekeepers of how much energy we give to the body.

In the same way that Swami Vivekananda said, "Do not make a religion of the kitchen," meaning, do not make food and eating a fetish; even more so, we should not put the body on the altar and worship it. The body is our instrument for operating on this physical plane, and like any instrument, like a vehicle, a computer, or a phone, we want to keep it in good operating condition so that it performs its functions well, and gives pleasure to its operator. We should cultivate the practice of knowing that the operator of the machine and the machine are not one and the same thing. In deepened meditation, we have a growing awareness of the great "I AM" within, beyond the body, even superior to the mind, and to the individual soul.

While living in the body, there are commonsense things we can do to keep the body-machine in good order: exercise and stretching, eating healthy foods (as Mother said, "Do not treat the body like a garbage can"), and thinking healthy, positive God-thoughts. I have experimented with different food regimens over the years with good results. In these past twenty-plus years, it became obvious that both gluten and dairy had deleterious effects on this body, so I gave them up.

Recently, I have been experimenting with Dr. Steven Gundry's ideas on focusing on the health of the gut, and its relationship with autoimmune diseases—in particular, the role of dietary lectins and their negative effects on our digestive system.

To have the right relationship with the body, to remain mindful of keeping the body healthy, and to do what is best for its smooth functioning, is wise. There is a line, though, where we do not let the body, and its relationship with the world, take control of our life. Affirm, "I have a body, but I am not this body," and give it its due, but no more. Let us practice finding that awareness that knows we existed before we took residence in this body and the awareness that knows we will exist long after this body has returned to dust. That while the body is important for accomplishing what we have come here to do, it is just an instrument for our use—a remarkable instrument, it is true, but just an instrument. I am pleased to have this excellent report from my medical team as it gives me the time and freedom to accomplish what God has me here to do.

A prayer:

> Every day, I pray for your perfect health, so that you too may enjoy that same freedom and ability to do all that your Soul has intended for you in this lifetime; that you use the gift of this marvelous machine, to manifest your highest nature, and to bring the Light of the Divine to this world through the instruments of your body, mind, and soul.

July 1

Touched by Saints

Two Saints we met while on the Road to Rishikesh.

I have had the great blessing to have been touched by saints in this life. I feel indescribable gratitude in thinking back on the grace that has flowed to me through these illumined ones. Memories streamed through my mind this morning, with several instances coming to mind from my first pilgrimage to India. The year was 1998. Phyllis had made it possible for me to travel on a pilgrimage to discover spiritual India. After a couple of initially disappointing days when we first arrived in Delhi and then went up to Haridwar,

I prayed to Babaji. I prayed to Babaji in the form of the Ganges, while lighting a little flowered candle boat and setting it adrift in the flowing river. I prayed that Babaji would show me spiritual India. Immediately upon arriving back at the hotel, Babaji arranged everything, beyond all expectation, to answer my prayer.[20]

As a result of Babaji's unfolding grace, I had the opportunity to meet wonderful saints, many of them unknown to the general public. They lead lives in quiet sadhana and radiate their grace to all. One saint that came to mind this morning lives in a hut near a leper colony. Due to language barriers, I do not know his name but came to understand that he was over 100 years old—he did not look even 60 years of age—as he wore little more than a dhoti, he was open to full inspection! He chanted Ram Nam, and he radiated such light and joy that I just wanted to stay with him in his hut. He came to mind this morning, and it would not surprise me to find that he continues living in that hut. In thinking of him, the touch of his grace came to me through just the thought of him—this thought brought me great upliftment. Time and space are not barriers to such a one, and his grace, oh so easily, transmits itself here and now.

Then, another two yogis with whom I came into contact with while on the way from Haridwar to Rishikesh bubbled up in my memory. Anand, a generous soul who took it upon himself to guide us while we were at Haridwar, knew of yogis living in a one-room apartment that was their ashram. What a feeling of purity I had when meeting these two souls. Swami Puruananda Giri, a disciple of Swami Sadananda Giri, himself a disciple of Master's, was the taller of the two—stately, withdrawn into himself, and radiating a beautiful presence. Then there was his brother disciple, though not a kriyaban. His name did not get recorded, but he chants Ram Nam, and oh what light and joy emanates from the

---

20   See *My Spiritual India* to read about ongoing other experiences.

core of his being. It seemed that Mother's own path came in the form of these two yogis living together, one practicing Kriya Yoga meditation, and the other chanting Ram Nam. Anand translated an interesting comment by the Ram Nam yogi. He looked at me and said, "You must have done a lot of spiritual sadhana in past lives in order to chant Ram Nam and practice spiritual sadhana, especially being all the way from where you live (in America)." I had not told him I chanted Ram Nam, so how did he know? You know, saints really are wonderful!

The "touch" of these saints did not come through physical touch, nor was it their words, as these exchanges were not laced with much conversation; rather, it was the touch of their being—the touch of God in them that transmitted itself, and continues to transmit its eternal message of purity, love, and joy that is God. I bow at the feet of these luminaries. They are not famous or known for attracting large crowds, but they know God, and give what they know freely, without constraint or thought of what saint you follow or organization you belong to—they give only because they see the God in you.

July 8

JULY 4TH

The lion and the lamb in perfect harmony.**

A revolution occurred in 1776—not simply a revolution of man against man, but a revolution of thought and of spirit. It was for an idea that had evolved thousands of years before but had been forgotten or ignored. We were gradually coming out of the dark ages, where superstition was prevalent, and despots, even occasionally somewhat benevolent ones, ruled the world. The newly evolving idea was a republic, a constitutional democracy that had a balance of power built in, and a Bill of Rights to protect the individual from the overreach of government. These were radical, revolutionary ideas, that had never been tried before in the remembered past—and most in the world at the time thought these ideas impractical.

This idea of constitutional democracy, with protection from mob rule, has now spread across this world, India being the largest democracy brought about by a non-violent revolution—although violence quickly ensued after its emancipation (it has been tough to escape the dark ages). Democracies, by their very nature, are noisome and messy—short-term efficiency comes from a dictatorship, but dictatorships come with self-destructive results, which have been repeatedly proven over these many centuries.

The outcome of this experiment in democracy has resulted in a country with many personal freedoms, prosperity, and an ability to adapt and change. It is a sad irony that some of the very ones who originally fought for their own freedom justified enslaving others. With a costly civil war, injustice was reversed, and while having equal rights for all citizens has taken time, and sacrifices by many, still, this form of government has shown the flexibility to adapt and change.

The key to any society surviving and thriving is for the vast majority of people to abide by the eternal truths that all religions have taught. The central commandments of Moses and the yamas and niyamas of Patanjali are best summed up by Jesus.

> Jesus said unto him, Thou shalt love the Lord thy God with all thy heart, and with all thy soul, and with all thy mind.
>
> This is the first and great commandment. And the second is like unto it, Thou shalt love thy neighbor as thyself.
>
> On these two commandments hang all the law and the prophets (Matthew 22:37–40).

Upon the principle of love for God, and for all those around you, hang all the laws and the teachings of prophets—this principle is so very true. We try to make up for the lack of observance of this most basic principle by writing more and more laws, wanting social justice, but often end up "straining at gnats while swallowing camels" (Matthew 23:24, adapted). With the result that laws upon more laws oftentimes do little to help us, and, instead, bring burdens to the majority.

If we want justice, then we must treat others justly; if we want respect, then we must begin by giving it. With every word and action, we create, then we reap, what we have set into motion. As Mother Hamilton said, this world is made up of individuals, and as individuals change, so does the world. We should not look to some grand scheme of a savior from above, but to the universal Savior within. All the laws from all the prophets hang upon what are ultimately deeply-held spiritual principles, and when a significant number of individuals act accordingly, this world will be a haven of peace, where the lion lies down with the lamb in total harmony.

Health Update: After the positive results of various scans by my allopathic doctor, I consulted with my new oncological naturopath, Dr. A. The naturopath seeks to create a healthy bio-environment that will produce perfect health in which such things as cancer cannot thrive. A primary diagnostic tool is taking specific blood tests to indicate imbalances in such categories as zinc, copper, and vitamin D—some 50 different measurements; these were taken before my second visit to the doctor. In all tested categories, I was in the desired range, and a few deserved a surprised "excellent" comment. He has subtracted a couple of supplements my previous naturopath had prescribed (he had studied with Dr. R., so they are on the same page in most things), and he added a few, such as green tea extract (filled with polyphenol antioxidants that reduce inflammation). One of our goals is to reduce inflammation and oxidation. He was pleased with my weight loss and approved my current food regimen. Onward with continued perfect health. He has extended the time I see him next to one year from now; meanwhile, I will continue with my current supplements.

July 12

LIVING FROM THE INSIDE-OUT

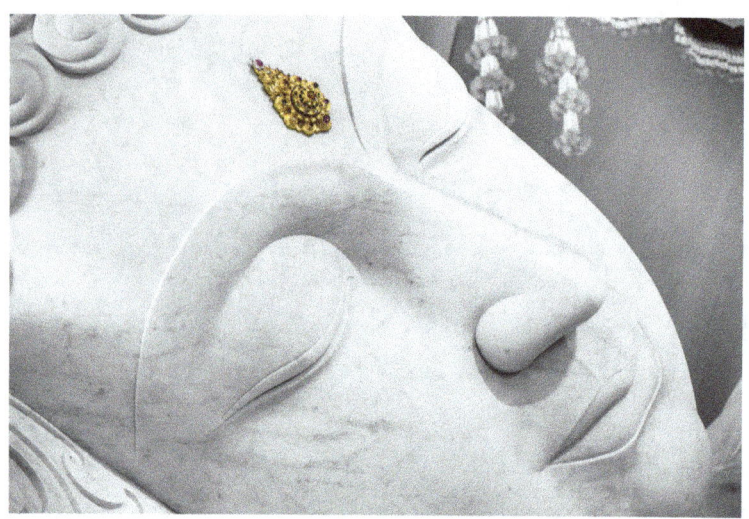

Sleeping Buddha with an awakened third eye.**

From the moment we open our eyes in the morning, our attention is drawn to what is "out there." The world is engaging, even compelling. The survival of this body, and the idea of our self, is defined by our relationship with the material world. So, it is not surprising that one of our most basic defaults is to identify with the body and its interactions with this world.

However, there is a fundamental flaw to this identification. The first, most obvious, fact is this body can be damaged, and it will eventually die—we are on an ocean, in a sinking ship, that, sooner or later, will disappear under the waves. The second lie: this is not who or what we truly are. In fact, who we are is so much greater than the body, and the world; those who have discovered this superior reality have sought to awaken us from what they say is a material dream-reality.

To uncover this greater reality is our spiritual journey, for this higher truth is what is called spirituality. To do this, we must open new ways of perceiving ourselves, and this world. Master taught us to focus on the spiritual eye, the point between the eyebrows. Since time immemorial, the spiritual eye has been known about and represented in art and lore. Spiritual scientists discovered that this third eye point is the doorway to the Kingdom of Heaven and that by focusing on it, we might open up this portal—we can ascend into that Kingdom, and its Light can descend into us. Then we realize that this world really is a dream-reality, and the Kingdom of Heaven is our real home, the truth of our being.

Through focusing on the third eye, and watching the breath, we suddenly feel uplifted—attuned to something higher than ordinary daily experience—in deepened meditation, and all through the day, we can keep this focus. We can cultivate the idea and feeling that the things of this world are passing phenomena. We definitely live in this world, but with this perception, we are not touched to the inner core of our Self by this changeable dream-reality.

All things are like the passing of the seasons. We have had a cool spring coming into summer; now we have sunshine and it feels good. But, the coolness of spring and the heat of summer are just passing events—we note them, but they do not define us. Sometimes, the world says we are doing well, and sometimes it finds fault with us; these, too, do not touch our core; it is simply information and passing phenomena. This body alternates from the enjoyable to the miserable; that is, more transitional bits of information. We now live in our core, from the inside-out—instead of how we lived in our past life, from the outside-in—outside-in is when we are defined by the body and its relationship to the world.

In the beginning, we focus on the third eye and cultivate dispassion for the things of the body, and the world. Then, we get glimpses into the actual experience; we become aware of this greater reality. Next, we pass through the jnani phase, where the world is continuously perceived as a dream, and the inner reality is far more real. As body and mind are purified, we gradually enter into the universal vision, in which we are aware of the Divine Nature both within and without. Oh, what a transformation this is! In one sense, our life is outwardly just the same, but inwardly, we are transformed. Life still happens, all of its ups and downs, and the body will still one day decay and die, but we are inwardly free—we are now established in our true Home.

July 13

PLANT PARADOX EXPERIMENT

Naughty baby Krishna and friends stealing curd.**

After the good reports I had from the allopathic and natu-
ropathic worlds, I wanted to give you a report on a
dietary experiment that Carla and I have been conducting
for the past seven weeks. I came across Dr. Steven Gundry online
and purchased his books: *The Plant Paradox Cookbook*, then *The
Summary Plant Paradox*. Since then, we have been following Phases
I and II, and are now entering phase III of this program.

The reason for the title *The Plant Paradox* is that while plants
are oftentimes a healthy food, not all plants or animal products
are good for the gut—the stomach, intestines, and colon. The

digestive tract is an emphasis for Dr. Gundry. It is what creates a healthy microbiome; the inner workings and health of the gut-digestive system.[21] If that goes wrong, then inflammatory disorders are created that can have serious health consequences.

Our societal foods and eating habits have changed very quickly in recent times. Dr. Gundry traces these "recent" changes further back than the Paleolithic period. Many of our digestive systems simply have not evolved quickly enough to accommodate these many new foods. Even the addition of what are generally thought of as healthy foods, like brown rice, corn, and beans, for instance, is not necessarily good for the gut.

Dr. Gundry was a world-class heart surgeon who had no training or interest in diet or supplements until he had a patient who, in six months, went from a 100 percent blockages in his heart down to a 50 percent blockage; this was an astounding turnabout. The only changes the patient made were to lose weight and to take supplements. It put Dr. Gundry on the trail of a scientific investigation into diet and supplements, which also led to a change in his own health habits: he lost 70 pounds, and cured the various ailments he had at the time. Since then, the doctor has been a convert, and now advocates dietary changes to effect good health and even recommends supplements, which he previously said only create "expensive urine."

---

21   Definition of the microbiome: Merriam Webster Dictionary. A community of microorganisms (such as bacteria, fungi, and viruses) that inhabit a particular environment and especially the collection of microorganisms living in or on the human body.

Microbiome Note: You have more microorganisms than human cells in your body. It is thought that your body has 100 trillion bacteria including other microbes. These microorganisms perform innumerable beneficial functions, without which you literally could not live. This mutually-beneficial relationship between human cells and microorganisms is considered healthy; whereas bad microorganisms inhibit the healthy functioning of the body; they take what they want without any beneficial return.

My experiment started seven weeks ago. Even though I was gluten and dairy-free (which, from many years of experimentation, I knew my body does not tolerate well), I was becoming stiff in my joints and waking up with headaches. When I read about Dr. Gundry's ideas, I thought it merited a try. Now, the good doctor definitely has a marketing plan going on with his line of supplements, but I was impressed by the amount of information he gives on his website and in his books, and he even suggests brands of supplements other than his own (his plan does not require supplements, but they are suggested for various reasons). With his eating plan, we limit the number of lectins we ingest through our food—lectins are proteins occurring naturally in plants that act as their protection (a poison) from being eaten by bugs and animals. Some plants contain more lectins than others, and those high in lectins can harm our digestive system. Plus, the widespread use of antibiotics by humans, and those used on animals, as well as various chemicals applied to plants, all have the potential to damage our digestive system. This damage to the gut results in our immune system kicking into gear to fight off what comes into the bloodstream that should not be there. This can create autoimmune disorders. The stiffness and inflammation I had in my joints, and congestion in my nasal passages, were definitely an out-of-control immune response—the way of eating outlined by Dr. Gundry promises to correct this.

Gluten, which I had long recognized as an agent that created stiffness in my joints, is one kind of lectin, but there are many more. In Phase I, we ate according to a simple list of yes foods and no foods for three days. After those first three days, we entered Phase II, six weeks in which the list of yes foods grows a bit. Tomatoes and night shades were out (I knew I should not eat these based on the Blood Type Diet, but I had grown lax in avoiding them); soy products were also out along with zucchini and yellow squash. However, there are many foods that are in the *yes foods*, and neither one of us has felt deprived with the new menu.

Results: the first week was quite easy for me, although it was definitely work—mostly for Carla to reorganize the kitchen and pantry and learn new recipes. It has also been fun to explore new ways of preparing food—the new recipes have been delicious (Dr. Gundry is obviously a "foodie," so his recipes are actually quite good). During the second week, I was having typical detoxing symptoms like sore muscles, and periods of tiredness; having been on many ten-day fasts, and other cleansing programs, I am familiar with these symptoms. On the other hand, I experienced increased flexibility, and at other times, I had a definite increase in sustained energy. The morning headaches disappeared almost immediately and, significantly, so did food cravings. There have been about four and a half weeks of detoxing, a longer period than I had anticipated. Carla has had these symptoms as well for almost the entire time. This past week, there has been a noticeable lessening of detoxing symptoms and the addition of smooth energy, as well as a fluidic flexibility in the joints (Carla said she has such fluid movement in her joints that it reminds her of when she took ballet). In addition, my nails are stronger, and I have improved digestion; very nicely, I have had a much-desired 6 percent drop in weight in the past seven weeks.

I look forward to even more improvements as we continue into Phase III. Phase III includes adding new foods—one new food a week, then tracking its effect. If no negatives are observed with the new food, then it can be added to the *yes food* list. In this way we tailor the foods we eat to our immune system's response. Dr. Gundry compares the work of healing the gut to gardening—we do not weed one day and expect a harvest the next. We weed out the bad bacteria in the gut by not feeding it the foods it likes and demands (cravings such as sugar, even sugar from carbs and fruit), and we fertilize the good bacteria with the nutrients they thrive on, such as leafy greens, high-quality fats, and proteins. We are experimenting with some of Dr. Gundry's supplements as well, a pre-biotic and *Vital Reds*.

There is nothing in this food program that anyone would say is bad or unbalanced; it is very healthy eating (it can be adapted to vegetarian-only, as well). The protests have mostly come from plant-based eaters who take exception to eliminating foods generally thought to be healthy. There might be others who are skeptical about how damaging lectins really are, but this program has a track record documented by a reputable surgeon who had a change of perspective triggered by real-life patients.

Dr. Gundry says in his clinics one in Palm Springs and one in Santa Barbara, out of the 800 patients with auto-immune disorders he has followed, all 800 have seen improvements by following this program. He does not expect this perfect score to continue as he does not think any plan can be 100 percent, but that is an impressive feat so far. I am not here to sell anyone on this program, but I wanted to share the results of this experiment with you and offer it for consideration. I will provide follow-ups as we continue this experiment on our quest for perfect health.

July 15

THE UNSEEN ELEPHANT IN THE ROOM

Lord Ganesha: Divine Elephant.**

Modern science has an unstudied phenomenon that, once it comes on the radar, will be one of those things that seem so obviously worthy of study that we will wonder why there was no recognition of it before. This phenomenon is all around us; in fact, it is fundamental to all existence; it is the life-force existing in all creation, what the yogis of India call prana.

In human beings, we sense this life-force, or the lack of it, in one another. Someone walks into a room, and they are like a spark plug that raises the level of life-energy in everyone. Then again, there are those who are like black holes, draining energy from the people around them. Creativity makes things happen, brings in new ideas, and awakens the feeling of God and the sacredness of life; all of these are products of life-energy. Everyone has some gift of this life-force to offer this world—some to a wider extent, others in a quieter way. We can feel this life-force energy in ourselves and others.

In the same way that we can sense this in people, so we can perceive it in nature. There are places in the world that stir life-energy: next to rushing water, we are invigorated; next to fetid, unmoving water, we sense its deadness. While walking through some forests, we feel the upright strength of the trees growing all around us, and in other places, we feel the sickly rot or burned-out hulks of a forest that is past its prime. Even in a sickly area, there are microbes and insects that feed off death, and prepare the forest for rebirth. There is a great deal of life-energy at work, even in destruction.

Mystics and yogis have long recognized the role of life-energy. Physical scientists largely focus on studying the sub-atomic and atomic worlds, molecules, microbes, insects, sap, photosynthesis, cellular functions, body organs, and interactions between life-forms. And while all these fields of study are fascinating, there is an elephant in the room most do not see—the life-energy that animates all the outward manifestations that can be seen under a microscope, through a telescope, or simply what is before our eyes. Those who have investigated the interiors of consciousness clearly see this elephant, and the elephant is the life-force.

Yogis have specialized for millennia in observation and conscious use of life-force prana. Master Yogananda brought to the West a rational understanding of this force, based on his own experience. He also drew on traditions explained to him by his great guru Sri Yukteswarji, who was in turn taught by Lahiri Mahasaya, who was in turn taught by Babaji. We learn that this life-force enters the body primarily through the base of the skull; from there, it enters the brain; thereafter, it is distributed throughout the body through the spine and nervous system. These physical mechanisms are the conduits through which life-energy operates, but the underlying force and intelligence is the prana itself.

In addition to the normal functions in humankind, and nature, prana plays an active role in the next evolutionary step of transforming the human into the Divine. In this area, the yogis of India are specialists. Master brought a refined technique called Kriya Yoga to the West. He writes:

> By the special technique of Kriya Yoga, the ingoing breath of prana and the outgoing breath of apana are converted into cool and warm currents. In the beginning of the practice of Kriya Yoga, the devotee feels the cool prana current going up the spine and the warm apana current going down the spine . . . When the Kriya Yogi learns to dissolve the ingoing and outgoing breath into a perception of the cool and warm currents going up and down the spine, he then feels his body as sustained by these inner currents of life force and not by their by-product of breath.[22]

This practice of Kriya Yoga awakens practitioners to the reality that they are made up of this life-energy; and further, an even more refined understanding leads practitioners to a subtler reality—all life-energy is Divine in nature, ringing out with qualities of bliss, peace, universal love, and light. Fortunately, we do not need to wait for the snail-like pace of physical science to discover all of this. We can explore these frontiers today in the laboratories of our own experience. As a practitioner of this science, even now as I turn my attention within, I am aware of the prana vitally

---

22   *Autobiography of a Yogi* (pp. 231–239), provides a definition.

vibrating throughout my body. I experience that this body is not a physical being as much as a life-energy being—not defined by the physical limits, but by its vast nature. Bliss fills this space, along with a freedom and a knowingness that I am part of all, and all is part of me. It is a seamless transition that is like a river moving smoothly toward the ocean.

We have been given a great gift. We must fully employ the means given to us so freely. We must make the most of this spiritual science for the realization of God by becoming living proof of what we have been taught. Know that we are truly made up of God-stuff, and then let us be a conduit through which the same power and intelligence that creates vast worlds is now fully operating in us. Help bring this world to its next evolutionary step; let us discover our true underlying divinity—nevermore being blind to the elephant in the room.

July 22

A SKILLFUL LEARNER

Yogacharya David being a skillful learner at Deer Park, Sarnath, India, 2005—the place where Buddha first taught his Four Noble truths. These grounds are filled with shanti-peace.

In Freud's psychological model, the super-ego is your conscience; it holds the ideals you have imbibed from your parents and the world around you. For many, these ideals can be completely over-the-top, meaning that you believe you should already know things and be skilled at doing things that you are not capable of performing. You cannot possibly fulfill these lacks, and they can act as a bludgeon, constantly hammering you. When in balance, and proportion, these ideals can positively make you aspire to, and achieve, great things in life. Aspiration is an asset; conversely, bludgeoning is bad.

To find the sweet spot in which you are energized for higher achievements but avoid a self-beating, you must pay attention to when you cross that line into self-castigation. This sweet spot helps you to balance capabilities and abilities; this requires a skillful learner. There are many areas in which you can become skillful, and due to karma, some come easier than others.

At an earlier time of life, I was backpacking around Europe. I ended up in the Canary Islands, living in a beach community. I was learning how to body surf using the human body like a surfboard. Finding a likely wave, I used my arms to paddle and gain speed so that I could ride the wave to shore. The air and water were warm, and it was fun to catch a wave and ride it in. I thought I was gaining some skill when a wave taught me otherwise. It was a great wave. I was on top of it, and it was really moving along. Suddenly, the wave broke underneath me, and I shot out past the wave into mid-air. I felt like a cartoon character that finds itself suspended in mid-air, knowing that it is about to take a painful fall. And fall I did, down on the hardpacked sand as the wave crashed down on top of me. My nose and arms were quite scraped by the force of the wave driving me into the sandpaper beach. Clearly, I was in an outdoor classroom, learning body surfing skills, and I was being taught a painful lesson by that wave.

Now, the super-ego could have beaten me up over making this mistake, or I could have blamed the wave for behaving as it did, or I could have fearfully never gone out again. The other alternative was to analyze what I did, consult with others, and learn to avoid such painful outcomes. I chose the latter and worked on identifying a wave that was about to break in the way mine had, and how to pull back at the right time. In other words, I became a skillful learner.

This option of being a skillful learner did not come naturally to me. Somehow, I came into this world with the idea that I should already know everything before I had a chance to learn it. It is a strange notion when you think about it, but it was strongly embedded in me. So, I would fake it until I made it, ashamed for anyone to see me taking learning steps. I could pick up many things quickly, which helped me maintain the illusion that I didn't need learning steps. And, if something did not come easily, then I avoided it. Of course, none of this really served me well, and most of all, it did not allow me the joy of beginning something new, making mistakes along the way, learning from the mistakes, and gradually becoming more skillful.

It took me a lot of years to learn to be simple and to have a child-like innocence when interacting with life. The spiritual field is fraught with ideals for the super-ego to plaster up on the mind's walls while holding up standards that do not allow for this process of learning. Again, it is wonderful and needful to have ideals to aspire toward in order to grow. But when those same ideals are used to bludgeon you for not living up to some perfection—they become harmful. To abandon your ideals is to stagnate, and to mentally self-flagellate yourself for not living up to those ideals is not only a waste of time and energy—self-flagellation is also a destructive force.

The idea is to be simple, sincere, dedicated, and to strive for your higher ideals while all the time being a learning machine—becoming more skillful in living up to those ideals with determination and a positive focus that allows you to grow in amazing ways.

Learn to identify that sweet spot where you hold up the highest and most transforming ideals, then be skillful in life—be right on the learning edge that yields the greatest benefit to you, and those around you. Sure, you must demand more from yourself, and strive to be more; this is absolutely necessary to make progress. But keep it positive, close to home, take joy when you note progress, and when you fall short of your lofty goals, take notes and learn from your experience. Learn with love and joy in your heart, and in doing so, you will draw invisible forces to aid you in fulfilling the tasks you have assigned to yourself in this life. You cannot make yourself perfect through self-will, but through valiant and persistent spiritual effort, you can touch the fabric of God's Being, and in touching Perfection, you are perfected; even as your Father in heaven is perfect (Matthew 5:48).

Note: We are currently guests of C. at the campground she manages on the Skykomish River. I would say we are camping, but with marble floors and granite countertops in our coach, it may give the wrong impression. The new term is called "glamping," glamorous camping. Be assured, it is the coach that is glamorous!

July 24

OM BABAJI OM

Yogacharya David: "Surrounded by pine trees
makes me dwell on Babaji—feeling he is near."

Babaji's spiritual state is beyond human comprehension,
Sri Yukteswar explained. The dwarfed vision of men cannot pierce to his transcendental star. One attempts in vain
even to picture the avatar's attainment. It is inconceivable.

—YOGANANDA

A t a time when we can understand so much of the physical universe, God places the inscrutable before us to remind us of the greater mysteries—those things that defy the mind's ability to take them in. The fact that Babaji maintains his body for hundreds, even thousands, of years is not his greatest mystery, nor is it the miracles he effortlessly operates; rather, it is what he has attained in his realization of the Infinite Spirit that would literally blow someone's mind if they were to take an unprepared glimpse at it.

From the *Autobiography*, we read.

> Opening the door, I saw a young man in the scanty garb of a renunciate. He came in, closed the door behind him and, refusing my request to sit down, indicated with a gesture that he wished to talk to me while standing. "He must be Babaji!" I thought, dazed, because the man before me had the features of a younger Lahiri Mahasaya. He answered my thought. "Yes, I am Babaji." He spoke melodiously in Hindi. "Our Heavenly Father has heard your prayer. He commands me to tell you: Follow the behests of your guru and go to America. Fear not; you will be protected."
>
> After a vibrant pause, Babaji addressed me again. "You are the one I have chosen to spread the message of Kriya Yoga in the West. Long ago I met your guru Yukteswar at a Kumbha Mela; I told him then I would send you to him for training." I was speechless, choked with devotional awe at his presence, and deeply touched to hear from his own lips that he had guided me to Sri Yukteswar. I lay prostrate before the deathless guru. He graciously lifted me from the floor. Telling me many things about my life, he then gave me some personal instruction, and uttered a few secret prophecies.

"Kriya Yoga, the scientific technique of God-realization," he finally said with solemnity, "will ultimately spread in all lands, and aid in harmonizing the nations through man's personal, transcendental perception of the Infinite Father." With a gaze of majestic power, the master electrified me by a glimpse of his cosmic consciousness.[23]

We live in a material age; therefore, we put great emphasis on the body, which includes the living body of Babaji. However, to merge into God means that you merge into the Source of His eternal Being, and into the inner Soul of Babaji. In experiencing your union with God, you know Babaji, Jesus, and the Soul of every exalted God-realized master.

Why do you want to come here to see this bag of bones? Focus your attention upon the Kutastha Chaitanya, the point between the eyebrows, and experience me directly.—LAHIRI MAHASAYA

Note: Where we are currently camped, we are surrounded by a forest of pine—Babaji said he feels most at home in the forests. These pines remind me of Dronagiri, where Lahiri Mahasaya met his great guru, and it seems I always feel close to Babaji in such forests, or when looking up at a vast vault of unobstructed stars. His beatific presence comes in an instant, lifting me into his purity and merging me into his spirit. What need do I have for more than this?

---

23   *Autobiography of a Yogi* (p. 336).

As I say, we put so much emphasis on the physical, but really, we have nowhere we need to go, no one we need to meet; we have only to go inside with full awareness and put our complete attention upon God and the masters, and we have all we need, and all that we will ever need, right inside of us. Master made July 25th a special Babaji Remembrance Day—this is good. And right here, right now, let us experience God and Babaji in full residence in our own heart and soul, truly remember him, and be one with him on this Babaji Remembrance Day.

July 29

Guru Purnima

Full Purnima Moon: first full moon in June
or July, a day to honor the Guru.**

Guru Purnima means to honor one's guru and guru lineage. Guru, of course, is not a word many of us grew up with, but it has entered the common lexicon since the 1960s and 70s. Now we have Wall Street gurus, communication gurus, and anyone who is said to be extraordinarily talented in their field can be identified as such. This generalization is not all inappropriate, anyone who brings light to a field of knowledge meets the qualification. However, the title takes on a more specific and refined meaning in the spiritual field.

A spiritual guru: one who brings light into darkness. He or she can be one who teaches a more intellectual course of study. However, it is the rare person of realization that can fulfill the true role of a guru. A realized being has risen to, and gained mastery of, the various spinal centers that represent specific levels of consciousness. The first chakra, or first energy center, concerns a basic quest for life and survival. Surrender of one's life in service to God, and to the God in humanity, is a means to rise above this initial level.

Then comes the desire for pleasure and the sex instinct that is meant for the survival of the species—this is nature's way of perpetuating humanity. Humanly, we can learn to imbue this energy with love, dedication, and beauty between a husband and wife, taking it out of the gross and indiscriminate nature into which it can devolve. But that same energy can be used for the higher purpose of gaining realization and being of service to God—rather than merely fulfilling basic urges and sense satisfactions. The transmutation of these energies is the key to attaining mastery over the second chakra or second energy center.

Climbing higher on the spinal ladder, we come to the evolutionary development of individual will. Here we learn to submit our will to Divine Will through spiritual dedication. Initially, an aspirant abides by spiritual laws handed down in religious traditions or through spiritual teachers. As the mind is purified, the direct intuition of Divine will becomes possible, and through submission to God's direction, spiritual mastery is gained in the third chakra, or third energy center.

The heart center signifies going beyond strictly individual concerns and growing into a larger world. Humanly, it means loving another and includes the willingness to sacrifice for others, a loved one, children, friends, or the larger world community: this center is a primer to Divine Love. Divine Love is experienced with the opening of the fourth chakra at the heart. There, Divine

Love can flow out to one and all in an unfettered way. The experience of Divine Love is purifying in itself and prepares the aspirant to give oneself, heart and soul, to Divine Love—transcending the personal/individual and entering the impersonal/transcendent.

The fifth chakra or fifth energy center concerns knowing the higher truth and right conduct. Initially, this is known through a quickening of the mind that makes us know that this is correct, and this is not. Submission in thought, word, and deed to this higher knowledge makes us activate dharma itself, and it prepares us for even more perfect attunement to inborn dharma—direct apprehension of truth. This attunement is our initiation for entering into the sixth chakra, otherwise known as Kutastha Chaitanya or Christ Consciousness.

In Christ Consciousness, there is a more perfect union with the Divine Mind. Love and intelligence are both informed by a steady stream from the pure Mind of Father-God. The individual is practicing perfect surrender in body, mind, and soul, and the power of God flows freely through such a one. In this stage, there is still the sense of "I and Thou," a thin but definite veil of division between human and Divine. The son of man, or human consciousness, surrenders completely to the Divine Essence and is willing to go through whatever God desires. Through these experiences in the Mystical Crucifixion, or in the Battle of Kurukshetra, the veil of separation is pierced—when the process is complete, there is only knowing the oneness of God.

This oneness is a merging into the seventh chakra or seventh energy center at the top of the head. The tall headgear or hats used in religions are symbolic of the fully opened seventh chakra. Depictions of the Buddha show three coils of hair above the top of the head, indicating mastery over the three bodies, the physical, astral, and causal: in other words, being established in this highest center. This is the summa cum laude for the yogi or spiritual master. Mother called this, "Going over the top." Once the individual has been completely subsumed into the spiritual, then the spiritual may once again manifest as the individual, only now it is all done in complete accordance with all the purity of the Spiritual Consciousness, manifesting through the human—the complete God-man or God-woman.

According to Meher Baba, anyone who is a master of the fifth chakra and above may function as a guru—not before. In some rare cases, the guru may have gone all the way, and having gone over the top, may serve to help others do the same. Large followings are not a sign of a more advanced guru; a Maha-Yogi such as Babaji, may only have a few disciples at a time, but all aspirants have earned their position—even then, their full realization is not guaranteed, for free will is always in play until complete illumination is achieved.

True gurus, such as Mother and Master, do what they do out of compassion and a desire to help others to know God. We are the direct beneficiaries of these benevolent Beings who spend their lives bringing spiritual Light to this world. Oftentimes, those who gurus seek to help are not able to fully take advantage of what they are given. But even though gurus want realization for all aspirants here and now, they also have the understanding that each soul comes with his or her own karma and purity of desire. A few may fully take what is given, others just a portion, and some may walk away empty-handed—not because it was not freely given, but because the individual was not yet ready to embark upon the Great Adventure.

So, we honor the guru and the guru-lineage for what we have been given. We make certain that we are not "the poor workman blaming his tools," but that we are ready to go to work and are fully engaged with the truth and the guru-shakti that the powerful guru gives. We strive to take the Light that has been freely given, and in return, we give the Light we now know within to all the world, sharing that Light in all that we do. For, to really honor the guru means that we do what he or she asks us to do, to give as he or she gives, to emulate the guru in all the important ways—to be an emissary of Truth. There is no greater way to honor the guru.

August 4

POWERING THROUGH STALL POINTS

Garuda is the eagle who carries Vishnu: his powerful
wings and clear purpose do not allow stall points.**

In the life of a sadhaka, there can come plateaus—times when it
seems there is no progress. This is a sign that you have run up
against an inner obstacle of some sort. Not all obstacles come
in the form of freight trains that run you over; many come in dark
whispers, or stuck energy; these signs are a call to action.

There are any number of reasons why you get stuck. Usually,
it entails a cooling off of your intensity in your spiritual practice,
combined with a vulnerable spot in your psyche. The simple fact
that you have separation from Divine Consciousness means that

you will encounter oppositional forces along the way. Some are mental, others emotional; some are physical/material. Most often, oppositional forces come in some combination of all three.

When an airplane is taking off, and has not yet gained enough altitude, a stall in power will cause the plane to drop to the ground like a rock. However, if there is enough altitude, then the plane can gain speed and recover from an impending crash. In sadhana, the aspirant may have a "drop-off in power" when there is not enough of a focus on spiritual practice to keep climbing. If there has not been enough progress gained, then ignorance clouds form around the devotee, and he or she crashes to the ground—it is as if there had never been a spiritual pursuit, to begin with, or it feels like it was a pursuit from some distant past. If the aspirant has gained enough spiritual altitude, then with renewed effort, he or she may start to climb again—and if the spiritual effort is not made, no matter the altitude, then that one will lose all that had been gained.

That is why, as soon as you are aware of being stalled, you must make a sincere and intense effort to put your mind back on God. You can sense the stall, and a lack of progress, when you feel inwardly neutral, or when there is a growing desire-nature for this world that outdistances your desire for God. When you are aware of these counter feelings, fiercely cut away all oppositional thoughts and desires the moment they show up, avoid temptations, chant God's name, and meditate until God-contact is made—these are the ways that you can power through a stall.

When your soul is once again humming in tune with Spirit, point out to yourself how real your current spiritual freedom feels. Compare this true independence to the ephemeral freedom the senses promised you. Work through mind scenarios in which the false premise of the senses leads you toward imprisonment in endless sense entanglements. Then feel the bliss and freedom of God, and compare these superior attributes to materialistic and sensual pleasures. Educate your mind to realize that the oppositional forces often come in the guise of a "friend," but in fact, they destroy lasting happiness, and bring you restlessness.

Full realization comes when every part of you knows God and there are no dark corners of opposition left. Then you can no longer stall or crash, for every part of you knows the truth, and you will never have even the slightest desire to trade that freedom for anything else—it simply makes no sense for you to do so, on any level.

August 5

Spirit Calls

Sailboat silhouette against a red sunset.**

M y Dear Ones,
There are times when I seem to be not quite of this world. In seeking to serve God and Gurus, I am finding They take me on diverse roads of Their own making. This poem below expresses some of what I experience, and what I most fervently want—that we all share in this heavenly kingdom that Mother, Master, Jesus, Babaji, and all great masters have come to inspire us to seek by sharing their Light with us. Even though I am not giving a talk this morning, know that I am with you in Spirit, and like the mariner in harbor who feels the power of the ebbing

tide and first senses the wind that will fill the sails, so am I pulled out to the ocean of infinite bliss.

SPIRIT CALLS

I soar upon wings of bliss;
Circumferenced never,
Open, clear, expansive, and joyful—
O, what remarkable freedom is mine!

It is the bliss long-sought, a freedom hard-won.
How many years in the making?
How many tears shed in sorrow?
Only to discover the keys to freedom
were in my hands all the time!

Now I soar and soar and soar.
Sometimes, my feet touch the ground,
Other times, I am born of the air—
No tethers, no gravity, and no limits.

Whether of the earth or of the air
I serve the Infinite One—
And with fire He scorches,
Removing ignorance from this world.

Dear ones, let us soar together, successfully fighting the worldly-gravity that binds. Let us be as one with our Infinite Beloved. For even now, the Song of Spirit is calling to us all.

August 9

THE FAMILY-ASHRAM

Mother Hamilton standing outside her
daughter Billie's home, Seattle, c. 1961.**

With these manifold activities, Lahiri Mahasaya sought to answer the common challenge: "After performing one's business and social duties, where is the time for devotional meditation?" The harmoniously balanced life of the great householder-guru became the silent inspiration for thousands of questioning hearts. Earning only a modest salary, thrifty, unostentatious, and accessible to all, the master carried on naturally and happily on the path of worldly life.[24]

---

24   *Autobiography of a Yogi* (p. 204).

Upon meeting his Sat-guru, Lahiri Mahasaya felt he wanted to stay in the Himalayas with Babaji and company, but his role was to be different—to prove to all that a householder, future father-to-be, and office worker, could also be a fully illumined spiritual master. Sri Yukteswarji also had a householder role for many years, as did Mother Hamilton. Each one faced the common challenge of how to balance an active life in the world, along with the requirement to maintain a spiritual discipline that deepens contact with God.

While each had their unique challenges, and each had their own ways of dealing with them, so did they rise to the challenge, and go all the way to complete realization. It is tempting to imagine if we did not have family responsibilities, how much easier it would be to focus on God, yet my pilgrimages around this world have shown me that monks and renunciants do not necessarily make great spiritual progress, even though that is their stated purpose.

Here is a question-answer time in one of Mother's Talks, when her daughter, a young mother at the time, brought up an important point:

Mother: Now, what are some of the other obstacles to keeping your attention upon God? Yes, Billie?

Billie: Being exhausted. (Mother's laughter here.) Meditation when your kids are still awake, or waiting 'til you're half dead and you're asleep.

Mother: Well, it is very difficult, I know, when you're raising youngsters and exhaustion is an obstacle. I've been through all these things, so I have understanding about them; but nevertheless, if your love for God and your Guru is great enough—and I include that because of what I experienced with my own Guru. My love for him was so tremendous! I was so **glued** to God in him that I was meditating upon his form, upon him, all the days of my life—morning, noon, night and in between. And I think

that I probably have lived one of the busiest lives that any-
body could. I was lucky if I got four and five hours of sleep
a night for years! I had children, too, and I had to go out
and work for 35 years straight. And it wasn't exactly what
you would call easy or simple to find time to meditate. So,
I learned to meditate through keeping my consciousness
upon God in my Guru—of loving him, of serving him, of
putting forth everything that I could to promote his work:
to speak to different people whenever I had an opening, a
foothold, and all this sort of thing.[25]

Marriage and family are essential parts of a healthy, functioning
society. We have seen the damage when families have not properly
formed, or from those that have not stayed together—damage to
children and adults, both. Having a spiritual core-connection to
the family makes such a difference. Although this does not guarantee all will go smoothly, it does promise that whatever individual and collective karma there is to go through will be greatly
helped when a spiritual core-connection is made and kept in the
family.

Children will ultimately respect what parents respect. It doesn't
mean that children will always follow their parents' spiritual path,
but a seed is planted in the child's mind that will remain—sometimes dormant, and sometimes coming to full fruition in this life.
We can think that spiritual parents will feel assured that children
will behave, be okay, and not have major obstacles, but that does
not respect the child's own karma that he or she came with or
free will. It is beautiful when children do feel a spiritual kinship
with their parents and family, but that is always an individualistic
choice. Even a spiritual seed that lies dormant in a soul for years,
or even lifetimes, will ultimately greatly benefit a soul—who

knows how many such examples we have had over many lifetimes that culminate today in our focus upon, and desire for, God alone?

Each of us must find our balance in family life, "to give unto Caesar that which is Caesar's, and unto God what is God's" (Mark 12:17, adapted). The aim: to love, and care for, those whom God has given to us, and all the while be free of the idea that "I am the doer," and free from attachment to outcome. What makes us know that we are making progress? It is the increasing spiritual freedom we experience even when discharging our worldly duties. Whether it is running a company, or washing the dishes, we feel God's Presence with us—His strength, joy, and wisdom, flowing through us at all times. The family home is our ashram, and just like a monk's ashram, the everyday chores must still be done: food selected and lovingly prepared, work done that supplies the food, shelter arranged, and much more. We must work through the rough edges of interrelationships that rub up against one another. Our home is our ashram, what makes it so is our love, dedication, and surrender to God.

Let us love the life God has given us, and while we can make plans to build a future that serves us perfectly, we can also love life in the process—what we have right here, in this place, and at this time. The love and gratitude for what we have now open the door for God to create, through us, all that He wishes to express in our life. And His will for us, even when it challenges us to our core, is, in truth, pure ananda-joy. His love, His wisdom-thoughts, and His bliss are not for some distant future in our life, but are with us even now, when we are fully open to it. This is what was discovered by Lahiri Mahasaya, Sri Yukteswarji, and Mother while living in their family-ashrams. This life is a voyage of God-discovery, and our family is not a distraction, but the very means by which we attain the universal vision.

August 12

ORGANIZED-CHAOS

The calm in the storm.

Aweekend with a house full of children, and Family Day on Saturday, is a reminder of a life of constant activity, children full of life-energy, and multiple things going on at the same time—in other words, what is, more or less, organized-chaos.

I have certainly lived with this full-time at earlier times in this life, and while I feel joy in such circumstances, I realize that it can make finding quiet times a challenge, especially for busy parents. Then, there is the problem of having such noise and life-energy all around you that can be so stimulating, and though you may dream of peace and quiet, the moment you have it, you find things to do to get things going again—there can be an addictive quality to being rajasic, always being stimulated.

To find a quiet-center-place within you, to be an observer and a witness to the play, all the while being a participant in life and playing the role you have been assigned, gives you internal balance. This quiet in the storm connects you with your breath and heart. Anxiousness and desire-nature disturb this inner equilibrium; hence, your task is to learn to attune mind and body to an inner-steady-calm. This should not be imagined as a seasonless life, one that knows no ups or downs—if that were the case, then you would not be participating in life, only observing it. But you can find a place inside that is the calm center, even as events are churning all around you.

This requires real spiritual practice. In moments during meditation, you may find it, then it begins to generalize to when you are participating fully in the world. At such times, a sudden feeling of peace fills you, and you realize, "This is one of those magic-moments." Love fills your heart and overflows to all the world. At such times as these, you touch *the hem of God*—fears and craving-desires subside—life is perfect.

Ah, to be in this state always is a dream come true. And, this is the promise of the spiritually illumined: the world is created out of the fabric of bliss, and it is also part and parcel of your innermost nature—it is yours to discover if you but make the effort to do so.

You need this balance in life: to be in the still-static state of inward calm and to be an active participant. In the stillness, you know your eternal connection with pure Spirit, God. From that oneness with God, you express God's fullness of Spirit in thought, word, and action, as you move from moment to moment in your life. That is why you put God first because when you create in life as God creates, you begin by being ensconced in Spirit, then

Spirit flows outward naturally as creation. When creation has fulfilled its purpose, then all form is withdrawn back into the Infinite.

One way to think of this: you begin your day in meditation, focus on God until you make contact, then enter into your day feeling peace and joy in your activities. At the end of the day: meditate on God, and withdraw all the day's activities back into God-consciousness. In this way, you replicate in a micro-sense what God does in the macrocosm.

You need not despair that you live in organized-chaos; rather, you need only find the balance in life that anchors you in the Divine—thereby giving your life a higher meaning and an inner source of joy that is not dependent on there being smooth waters around you. It is veritably God living His life in your form, and He loves the life He creates, for at each stage of creation, He pronounced, "It is Good." To truly know this, you must, of course, be in harmony with His will. As you thus harmonize, you will find that you are truly made of the fabric of God, and it is so woven into your being that you and He are inseparable—even in the midst of organized chaos.

August 17

TREVA KOLER

Treva Koler with Yogacharya David, 2015.

Earlier this week, our dear Treva Koler left the body. Treva was the mother of Reverend Larry Koler and a kriyaban; she has been a member of our Seattle Group for these past forty years. Treva has seven children, and a recent family gathering counted nearly forty family members; amazing to think, from two to 37 in a lifetime. Treva was 90 years old when she peacefully passed, surrounded by family. Until the end, she had an active intelligence and keen awareness.

For the past many years when seeing Treva after a Service, she always approached me with a beautiful smile, and I felt God's great love flowing through me for her. She always had some piece of news she had seen in the papers or on television that she found interesting and spoke of with animation, or she would cut out some humorous cartoon to share with me that she found funny and insightful. When she first came to Mother Hamilton, Mother would often observe with admiration that Treva had raised her seven children—for many years she did so on her own, due to circumstances outside her control. Mother, herself a single mother of three for many years, spoke very highly of Treva. Most of her children went on to earn college degrees and became successful adults—a great achievement.

Treva performed a wonderful service for us when she drove to Shoreline and Mt. Vernon to help Carla organize Mother's Talks. We were in the early stages of getting Mother's Talks ready for publishing, and Treva's commitment and organizing skills made a significant contribution to that end—methodically sorting, labeling, and checking titles against lists. She would arrive, and after we had some pleasant conversation, she would get right to work and be steadily at it until Carla prepared lunch, then she would continue working steady until it was time to go. She was conscientious and detailed and could be relied on to keep things sorted—attributes I am sure she honed while working for many years in a doctor's office.

I do not think Treva would mind my sharing an experience she once had. While giving birth to one of her children, Treva died. Between the time she died and was revived, she had what is now called a Near Death Experience. During the time her body was dead, she found herself in a beautiful field. She felt it was so perfect that she never wanted to leave. Then she thought of her small children who needed her, and with great reluctance, she knew she needed to return for them; at that moment, she was aware that she was back in the hospital room, and she heard the doctor say, "She's breathing again!" She thought to herself, "Oh, shoot!", sorry to have left that place of peace and beauty.

Like many who reach the autumn and wintertime of life, Treva had a persistent question, "Why am I still here?" It was a question that did not leave her alone and speaks to something we all must wrestle with. For many years, it can seem our lives follow along a certain track: education, work, raising a family, and looking to accumulate enough to see us through the rest of our lives. Treva always had a strong desire to do what was correct, a moral and dharmic sense for right action. So, when life became less about doing for others in the family and at work, it left the question, "Why am I here?" Which relates to the questions: "Who am I?" "Is there a purpose beyond these normal tracks of life, which can seem to run out before physical life does?" Ultimately, these are spiritual questions, and those we can greatly benefit from asking, by making an inquiry into the deeper self, and finding an answer from that deeper Self—sooner, rather than later.

I will miss our dear Treva whose bright and inquiring mind always brought forward some new subject, her willingness to serve, and whose legacy of family will carry on far into the future. I know she was ready to move on into her new life, and she will be surprised by how many there are to greet her in welcome. She was looking forward to seeing her father once again—she is greatly loved by many—both on this side of the veil and on the other.

August 19

PURPOSE

Mother Hamilton: A shining Light of Purpose, 1960s.

Knowing our purpose in life is a remarkably important thing to realize, and to fulfill—for purpose is closely tied to life itself. Every soul has taken incarnation with purpose—its intention for ways to live, grow, and learn. If anyone becomes divorced from his or her purpose, then a crisis is induced—it may be a full-scale, life-threatening crisis, or a simmering undertow that is a drag on energies and an inner sense of fulfillment.

Purpose does not necessarily mean something lofty, or otherworldly. For many coming into this life, their purpose is very down to earth. I had friends in high school who knew exactly what they wanted to do in life: be a welder, a truck driver, get married and raise a family, be a physical therapist, a lawyer, (one friend traded stock on paper because he had no money to invest at the time), a doctor, etc. Then there were other kids who were much more general in thinking: go to college and then figure out their purpose, go to work for one of the better-paying companies nearby, or, after high school, take a job based on what is available. And some kids stumbled down into dark places with alcohol and drugs, having little direction other than to get high.

It seemed everyone had some kind of purpose they were pursuing—except, perhaps, for me, and I was in crisis. Since I seemed to be alone in the crisis, I kept it to myself and continued to do some of the things the world expected of me: such as work, and college. My father had dreamed of going into the business that my grandfather had started, and he did—he was one with a strong sense of purpose in life from the start. For me, it is strange to say, the world did not seem to offer what I needed. But I lived in this world with its demands for survival. There was no other vision or world in my sights at the time.

In hindsight, I can see that I was drawn by a guiding intelligence that gradually revealed my purpose. At first, it was an inarticulate knowing, through sporadic experiences, which started to form into something more focused. My Guru drew me to herself, and she gave me the template for a blazing purpose, much of which was far beyond my grasp at the time—she was both a distant guiding star and she lit the ground in front of me so I could take learning-steps into a new world.

My purpose was not more important than that of my friend who was to become a welder, my father who grew a business, or others who were in step with their true purpose in life. What is important, even essential, is that each person is in step with his or her own purpose and that this purpose is life-affirming and growth-producing. There are those whose choices lead to dark places that are neither life-affirming nor growth-producing—these individuals become lost souls that may wander in self-produced kinds of hell, moving from one painful existence to another until that pain induces them to reconsider their choices and move toward the light of the positive purpose inherent in all souls. Ultimately, every individual is led to the Light of his or her own soul—as Elizabeth Haich said, "Eternity is long enough!"

Others may live lives pulled along by the current of the world, doing what others do, until they come to a point where they realize that they have lived their lives according to the expectations of others. They do not really know their true purpose. For some, purpose changes in life, and what had been a clear purpose earlier, now no longer fits. This change can require painful adjustments at the time to keep in sync with the soul's purpose.

Happy is the person who is in harmony with his or her soul's purpose. Knowing and living out that purpose does not mean there are no challenges; quite often, it is just the opposite. A clear purpose may intentionally put us into situations that stretch us to the utmost, but we are exactly where we are meant to be. Nor does it mean that, from a worldly standpoint, we are an outstanding success. Krishna told Arjuna to engage in the battle, and even if he is killed on the field, he is a spiritual success because he is doing what he had come to do. Sometimes, being in harmony with purpose collides with what others think we should be doing, and that collision may result in disappointment, hurt, and anger. This cannot be helped when we are obeying our true purpose. We may trust that when it comes to fulfilling our true purpose, it will ultimately be for everyone's highest good.

To know and follow our true purpose is the greatest adventure, for the soul's ultimate purpose leads us to our spiritual Home—God-realization. For those who are awakened to this spiritual purpose, there is no reason to stand in judgment of those who are seeking to fulfill more earthly goals, as long as that is their true purpose—we can take joy in seeing that other souls are seeking out what is truly theirs to do. Just as we can affirm that, even when our soul's purpose takes us out of the common ways of this world, we are exactly where we need to be, and may rightfully feel joy in knowing that we are fulfilling our true purpose.

August 26

PHASING IN TO GOD

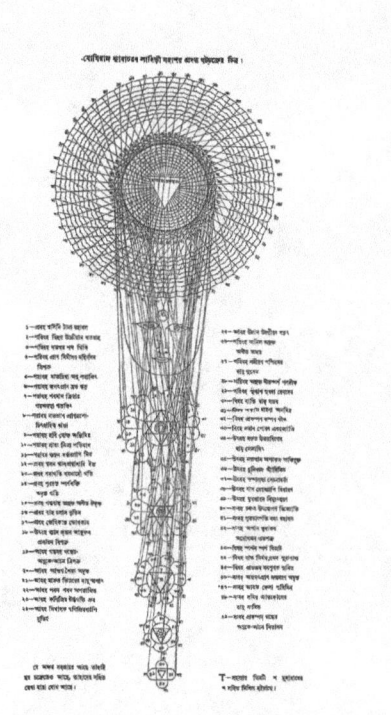

Lahiri Mahasaya's drawing of the chakras that represent
the three bodies connecting to Supreme Consciousness.

There are advanced stages of meditation in which consciousness effortlessly synchronizes with any one of the three
bodies, or beyond. Self-mastery offers the freedom of moving one's awareness between these three bodies with ease. An
intellectual may do this when he or she loses awareness of the

physical body or is only vaguely aware of it while performing a thought experiment. A healer may be aware of life-energy as it moves through in waves or currents from the healer's body to the healed. The spiritual man, or woman, can transition through the physical, astral, or causal bodies, and enter a spiritual state of Being that is beyond all three lower bodies.

These bodies, and the spiritual state I speak of, are not merely theoretical, but practical, and very real experiences that are known to the advanced spiritual scientist. Master spoke of the ability to concentrate and said that concentration is required for success in any field of endeavor. One may learn to concentrate on any subject of study, and when concentration is used to focus on God, it is called meditation.

One does not usually need training to focus on the physical plane of consciousness, for this is the ordinary state of most people on the planet. When someone wishes to learn to meditate, he or she is challenged with memories and projections of the mind from this material plane as daydreams. Suddenly, you are thinking of what happened before and what may happen in the future in this world. Imagination, or the ability to create mental images, may also become creative and generate imaginative daydreams.

By the continued practice of meditation, you may be aware of the life-energy in either a static form, as your astral body, or kinetic motion. As an astral body, you are filled with a wonderful, vibrating hum of life-energy units, or life-trons, that make up your astral form. Consistent with life-energy, creating a form or a body, it also flows directionally or multi-directionally. This life-tron, or prana, is responsive to your will, and also has an intelligence of its own that can dictate what it does and where it goes. Artists, healers, and musicians are often aware, to some degree, of life-trons and are inspired by their astral body and its use of life-energy.

As concentration advances in meditation practice, one becomes aware of the idea plane of consciousness. Here, deep concentration takes the practitioner beyond the physical preoccupations of this world, and beyond the energy-astral body. There are many theoretical scientists that can perform thought experiments in which various scenarios are thought out. A theoretical thought experiment can then be tested in some form, and the accuracy of the experiment can be verified. Builders, engineers, and creative types of all walks can be proficient in shifting to the idea realm. Einstein was famous for stopping in the middle of doing something and phasing out of the material realm and into a thought-field wherein he performed a thought experiment—oftentimes, to the bewilderment of those around him.

The spiritual scientist's aim is to go beyond these three bodies or states of consciousness. The physical, astral-energetic, and causal-idea bodies are seen as barriers to the entry into a supreme state of Being. The advanced practitioner may instantly phase out of the physical body and phase into the spiritual. Here, the limits of the three bodies no longer pertain; rather, there is an expansive freedom in which even an idea is limiting. This freedom is pervaded by a feeling of purity, and while thought is transcended, awareness is very much intact. In this purity is a sublime exaltation—bliss is all-pervasive. So, expansiveness, purity, bliss, and pure awareness are the realities of this spiritual state of being or God-consciousness.

In this state, the constantly restless nature experienced in the lower three bodies finds rest in perfect equilibrium. After being in this high state for some time and enjoying this bliss, a thought may come from that highest consciousness. Only now, the thought does not create restlessness; rather, the thought is in perfect harmony with the highest divinity. From this thought, life-energy may flow as creation, and thought and life-energy may move through the physical body. In all three bodies there is a knowing connection that comes from the highest state of consciousness—a phasing in of the spiritual still-state of the highest consciousness that expresses itself in one, two, or three of the lower bodies. The eyes open, and the same astral, causal, and spiritual states are now all seen as manifesting in the world as all there is—God is known to be all-pervading.

This phasing out of the three bodies in meditation is necessary in order to rise above the three bodies, so to be established in the highest God-consciousness. Once that is attained, if Divine Will wishes it so, then that highest Source of all that is creates through you by actively manifesting in the three bodies. God creates through you, and as a result, you maintain your connection with God, even while living in a physical body. In this way, the spiritual scientist proves through practical experience that one may be on intimate terms with creation, and be one with God.

August 31

TEST EACH SPIRIT

Mother Hamilton, Los Angeles, mid-1970s.

am reading through a transcript that Carla had highlighted for me in which there was a question-and-answer format Mother was engaging us in. The year was 1986, and I asked Mother:

> David H.: Mother, how can you tell when the impressions, and the voice, and the feelings, that you're getting are from God and not just from yourself?

> Mother Hamilton: Well, you all remember that in the Bible it says, "Test each spirit as it comes, or each thought, because not every spirit is of God." You have intuition

inside of you. You intuit. In other words, that is God speaking to you. I have used that many, many times in my lifetime. And your solar plexus is your second brain and that's where you get the feeling that something is right or wrong. So, when you don't feel totally comfortable, and don't get the green light on something, take a good look at it. I had that happen to me when I was in New York. I was shown something that I could do, that I wanted to do very badly, and it looked like a beautiful arrangement.

Then I remembered, "test each spirit as it comes." I did that, and immediately I said to God, "If that's right let me know but if it isn't, show me something else." Immediately, I got a totally different picture. And I would have been in deep trouble if I had done what I first got. So, when you get these feelings of either go ahead or the stop signal, listen to them. Don't go against them. That is God in you, protecting you, guiding you, directing you.

In reading this, I noticed that Mother did not give a concrete reference, such as, "look it up in this book," but rather gave a means for going deeper inside myself and communing with God. The other thing that struck me was that Mother actually gave an example from her own experience in which she had misleading directions, some action that seemed so right in her own mind, but God prompted her from within to "test each spirit."

It is amazing to think that 32 years have passed since Mother said this. I think back over the many experiences God had yet to put me through, and the times when I both honored and ignored Mother's sage advice. I do wish I could say I always exercised the precise discrimination Mother taught, for that would have saved me a lot of pain and trouble.

However, the relevance of her teachings is timeless, and not just for me, but for us all. Let us remember to take the time to really go to God to ensure the direction in which we are heading, and to confirm that the day-to-day decisions we are making are in concert with the highest light and wisdom of God. It is crucial to our long-term happiness and fulfillment that we really listen to what Mother taught and do as she did.

September 2

FILLED WITH THE BLISS OF GOD

Swami Ramdas (Papa) had a spigot of bliss on his big toe!

Continuing from the previous post, *Test Each Spirit*, this includes another excerpt from a talk Mother gave in 1986. I had the privilege of asking Mother another question close to my heart:

> David H.: You go through many experiences when you are on your way to God. At what point do you fully know that you and God are one? In other words, how do you know when you've completed the journey?

Mother Hamilton: Well, you know that you're living in a dual world, but you're filled with the bliss of God. You feel that you're full of God. You feel like when Ramdas came out of the cave at Arunachala in India, he'd been there for 20 days. He ran about, embracing the trees and every man he could see. So, this man he embraced said, "You're in the upper story, eh?" He said, "Ramdas is in all stories." Anyway, he was great in God and full of fun. He enjoyed the world. He wasn't just sitting there, pretending he was God and that everybody should bow at his feet and worship him. I've told you before that he said, "Ramdas has trouble with all this head bumping when people come and put their heads on his feet to pay their respect to him." He says, "Ramdas doesn't know if they're trying to get God from him or give him a present from God. He has a big spigot on his big toe and when they put their heads down there, he turns the spigot and gives them a shot of spirit and they go away happy." He was a lot of fun.

It is a rare privilege to have the opportunity to ask a fully realized master about the ultimate attainment of full God-realization. There are many steps or levels of realization, all of them wonder-filled in nature, but the supreme attainment is only known, and can only be explicated, by a true spiritual master who has achieved this rare state. Even then, to have a spiritual master who is willing to directly comment on this exalted state is a true moment in time to be treasured.

Mother's first measurement for complete God-realization is the ability to both live in the world of duality and be filled with the bliss of God. This mirrors Sri Yukteswarji's statement that God-realization is ever-new joy—to know within you, "I am living in that blissful-joy, feeling God's Presence, day and night without a break." Then Mother went on to refer to Papa living in a cave on Arunachala Mountain after receiving the darshan of Ramana Maharshi, during which time he was chanting Ram Nam, day and night. Coming out of that cave, Papa saw that the whole world is God, and everyone in it is His veritable manifestation. Papa's joy was overflowing; it penetrated into everything he did and everything he saw.

Oh, what bliss was Papa's; what a pure state of realization was coursing through and through him! And finally, Mother spoke of the fact that such a fully God-realized soul is a blessing to all who come into contact with him or her—with a big spigot, Papa issues out bliss to all who seek his blessing! Papa's bliss is infectious; it is positively maddening! For such a realized soul is truly a fountain of joy, and lives on earth to lift one and all into this universal vision.

September 13

Loon Lake Retreat:
A Meditation on Swami Ramdas

Mother Hamilton and Swami Ramdas (Papa)
in Bhajan Hall, Anandashram, India, 1957.

The Loon Lake Retreat has turned into a lovely bi-annual time to focus more deeply on a particular aspect of sadhana. This recent retreat was a meditation on Swami (Papa) Ramdas, a perfectly realized master who attained Sahaja Samadhi—sahaja means a natural state, no effort is required to maintain this level of awareness, and samadhi means ecstatic union with God. The aspirant for this union performs sadhana, intense spiritual practices that purify the body and mind and prepare him or her to be in oneness with the universal Spirit. Papa had performed this sadhana to perfection. He wrote about his experiences in a number of truly remarkable books, including *In Quest of God* and *In the Vision of God.*

We connect the thread of Papa's life as it wove itself into the life of Mother Hamilton. By 1954, Mother had attained a high state of realization, Nirvikalpa Samadhi: union with God that is unwavering, where the devotee has the ability to move in this world in a normal way, but the perfect union still comes and goes. Mother knew there was a higher state for her to attain, but her guru, Paramhansa Yogananda, had left the body in 1952. With an ongoing intensity for God that was like someone who could not breathe and was desperate for air, she prayed to God that either He reveal Himself to her directly or send her someone who could help her to gain the final mile of realization. God replied to Mother, "I shall meet you face-to-face, that our joy may be full."

While Swami Ramdas was on a world tour, Mother came to know that Papa was to be in Seattle from a fellow minister of Master's, who asked Mother to accommodate Papa in whatever way she could while he was in Seattle. Upon meeting Papa, it was ecstasy at first sight. Later, when Papa said to Mother, "God has come to visit God," Mother knew it was the fulfillment of what God had promised her months ago when He said, "I shall meet you face to face." Thus, God orchestrated a number of events that eventually took Mother to Anandashram, Papa's abode of bliss.

During our retreat, we saw Papa primarily through Mother's experiences as she had written and spoken about them. We took those events and meditated upon certain aspects of them—for instance, Mother seeing an effulgence of Light emanating from Papa's body that went out as far as her vision could see. We focused on that Light in meditation, attuning ourselves to that very same universal Light, and making it our own. It was a blissful time spent together, while working individually.

I am only sorry that all could not be there who would have liked to have been. However, even now, there are no limits to our joining together in meditating upon that Light of Papa, of Mother, and of the universal Lord of creation. We can merge into that Light and make it our own. We are completely free to yearn for God, even as Mother felt such a great desire for union with God and Guru. God's bliss lives in every particle of space, and it lives in us. Let us take the lead from Papa, from Mother, and from the great Ones who have gone before us to help us know that union with the Beloved is our rightful inheritance. He awaits us so that we might turn to Him so that He can embrace us, and make us His own. This is the message of Papa, of Mother, and of Master. Be it so!

September 16

HONORING YOUR SEASONS

Tree of all four seasons.**

Septebmer has always been a time of new beginnings for me; perhaps it started with it being the commencement of a new school year. But it is not just that, all through my adult years, I have noticed it to be a time of launching a new phase in my life. While nature around me is in harvest and preparation for winter, I have a springtime of new generations being planted.

This September, we are also experiencing a harvest: finishing renovations to the house; we are now sporting a first-floor apartment and Rebecca is moving in. It is always interesting to be eyeing up the completion of a larger project, an additional rush of energy to complete what had been started some time ago. With this completion of a project in sight and the newness of a "sadhaka in the side-door," I also feel there is something new with the Work I do for God and Gurus. It is now in the seedling stage, but I feel the hallmarks of its coming.

Every life has beginnings, times of growth, and then the harvest or completions built into a natural rhythm. However, many of us live lives insulated from the seasons. We work indoors and have jobs that do not reflect changes in nature (50 weeks of regulated hours with two weeks of vacation). This can make us insensate to what should be a natural cycle for the body, mind, and soul. This comatose sense of sameness makes us dull to the miraculous life occurring all around us.

We thrive best when, like a farmer or gardener, we feel in sync with the seasons. In sync with the timing to prepare new ground and sow seeds, to water and fertilize those seeds, to watch them sprout and grow into the light, to gather the fruit of those labors in a grateful harvest, and then finally to enter a winter-time rest. In that time of rest, we focus on the still-state from which all creation comes. And, when God is ready, new cycles of growth begin anew. Of course, life does not always operate in such defined beginnings, middles, and ends as a farmer's life does, but if we pay attention, we will see such cycles operating in our lives.

God creates in us, and we feel a stirring when something new is coming forward. New beginnings are exciting times of discovery, a fresh energy coming into life. Some people hold back from new beginnings because they threaten the status quo, but this blocks the renewal of life—fear becomes a terrible denial of life. Some are good at beginnings but are not steady in cultivating that new growth, unable to sustain the energy over time that is required to bring the creation to fruition. Drawing upon inner strength and determination, we can overcome all obstacles and bring the creation to its natural completion. In harvest, we celebrate and taste the fruit of creation—we feel the fulfillment of what has been brought about. Some do not take the time for this acknowledgment and celebration but are busy, off to the next thing. It is important to take the time, even as God does after each stage of creation. He stands back and says: "It is good." Then comes wintertime rest, deepening contact with God in the still-state, drawing from the all-powerful Spirit, renewing our soul, and preparing ourselves spiritually for a new season—to dream new dreams.

Our inner spiritual life also goes in such cycles. So, do not become dulled to new life surging forward in spiritual practice. Be sure to put in the hard work to increase those sacred seeds in their growth; reap the harvest of peace, bliss, and joy. Then let us merge our little self with the Supreme Self in complete stillness. Our spiritual life reflects, like all of life, these cycles—let us stay alive to our own rhythm of growth so that we may reap God's great harvest.

September 20

The Hero's Journey

Ram returns to Ayodhya from his hero's journey.**

Everyone loves a good story, whether told orally, in a book, or a film. And the best stories entail the hero's journey. Such a story portrays the hero being drawn to a course of action, often taking it reluctantly, an action in which he or she must leave all that is known and familiar and set out to accomplish a noble and selfless goal. The nature of such a story is such that it entails the risk of death or actual death, and then an eventual return, or rebirth, and the attainment of something new, better, and more expansive. Carl Jung called characters and themes found in hero's journey stories "world archetypes"—so pervasive and enduring are such stories that they belong to the collective unconscious.

Powerful stories can carry us places, even as does beautiful music—which is its own sort of storytelling. It can be useful to see our life as a living narrative, to see it as a hero's journey. The hero seeks out truth and is willing to go anywhere, and do anything to attain what he or she is seeking. We can certainly see this pattern in Mother's life. As we studied her time with Papa during our last retreat, or in the story of her meeting her master, Paramhansa Yogananda, we saw that she was inspired to fulfill something she had always known she was to do, a destiny that was important not only for herself but for the world at large. This knowledge, that she had a calling, something she must do, something that must be realized, drove her beyond all reason and caution to journey into higher and higher states of consciousness—to her full God-realization.

We can think that such stories are only true for great spiritual masters such as Mother, Papa, or Master, but that is not acknowledging that God is the indwelling Presence in everyone. As Master once said, "The same God that is in me is in you." What a wonderful truth for him to confirm, a fact that is true for all creatures—for God is the seed-force in one and in all. In truth, God is the driving power behind everything we think, say, and do, whether it be mundane or spiritual. For, everything in our life is orchestrating events so that we might come to our ultimate hero's journey.

There are many journeys of a hero's nature that we experience over time. It can be a simple thing, such as telling the truth when it would seem easier or more expedient to tell a lie. Or, it can be a more difficult test, doing something that is the right thing to do, when doing so can cost a great deal. Best to create a pattern for ourselves for when we face a difficulty and overcome fear: we do what is right, whatever the potential cost. As a result, we grow stronger, and the integrity of our soul shines out. Ultimately, we are being purified by such experiences—prepared for the final mile of God-realization.

Whether we find ourselves on the first rung of this story or on the final mile, the pattern we follow is the same—we stay true to the higher light of truth, love, and universal service in all we think, say, and do. As happens in any hero's journey worth its salt, the hero may fail to live up to the standards of the noble path along the way. But the hero does not give up; rather, he or she recovers and keeps going—that is what makes it a hero's journey. And that is our hero's journey: we recover, and we keep going no matter what. It is the sure way through darkened places and into the light. We are here to individually and collectively, walk upon the path of the hero, to make our way to the portal of the Infinite, to enter into that portal, and then to go beyond all that we have known before. In truth, **our** life is the greatest story ever told; so, make it a good one; make it count.

September 23

DIVINE COMMUNION

Yogacharya David reading to Swami Satchidananda
and devotees, Anandashram, India, 2007.**

Who is my mother, brother, or sister? Those who are actively attuned to my Heavenly Father—pure Spirit, beyond time and space, beyond personhood—they are my spiritual family, this supersedes all other relationships (Matthew 12:48–50). In saying this, Jesus was making an important point to those around him. Even the special bond of the eldest son to mother is secondary to spiritual communion with God.

I watch as the nearly full moon descends into the western sky. It is a September harvest moon, in its radiance. I feel an even greater after-glow from yesterday's equinox group meditation. What glory there is in divine communion, not only with our

Heavenly Father/Divine Mother but also with all brothers and sisters coming together in spirit. This superior union in Spirit connects us all and is greater than bonds of blood, greater than friendships based on common worldly interests, for it goes to the innermost core of the Atman or Soul—my part of God.

The infinite Lord has been teaching me the nature of this spiritual bond over these many years. When I sat at the feet of Swami Satchidananda, he said at the time of my departure—after spending four months at the Ashram—"Whenever you think of the Ashram, you will be here." I had some notion of what he was saying, but really, I had only touched the surface of those deep waters to which he was alluding.

Through deepening experience, new ways of connecting with not only the Ashram and Swamiji, but with all God's creation, began to reveal themselves to me. Truly, I could think of Swamiji halfway around the world and I did feel that I was with him. This form of connection is different from a psychic connection—in which I know something about someone through intuition. I asked God to take that (psychic connection) away from me because I could feel its allure to my ego-sense. No, this connection happens in a Divine Field. In knowing God-experience, I also commune with whatever God reveals about different ones He brings to mind. In this field, there is no ego allure, just a deep feeling of a compassionate, loving, Spirit.

Information coming from this inner communion varies according to Divine Will: from specific information to a general sense of being, from past life influences to what may occur in coming times. No curiosity or delving into more than what is given is triggered by such inner communion but a very simple trust that whatever comes to me is what is needed in the moment. Physical proximity is not a requirement. Spirit is a time-and-space annihilation. Communing through Spirit operates through a substratum present in all creation. In Spirit, everything exists equally, without distinction of high or low or the many opposites that occupy material relationships. Really, when it comes down to it, there is no such thing as brother or sister, mother or father; there is only one Being who is perfect, pure, and all-pervading—all expressions are of this one Spirit. Therefore, I am really only knowing something about my Self, for there is no other.

As we sat in meditation on this powerful equinox, inwardly communing with infinite Spirit, various disturbances that others were experiencing effortlessly came to my awareness—for I feel no difference between various parts of God. Physical discomfort, emotional pain, or blockages, and restless thoughts, all dance across my mental screen. And what do I do with these? I pass them on to the feet of God, I surrender them to Him. It may be something from those sitting in the room with me, it may be from those who are at a great physical distance—in Spirit, it makes no difference. There are times when the pain or disturbance is excruciating, but it is all God, and therefore it is all good. It is all about surrendering to the Light, meaning letting go of all that keeps us from knowing our oneness with God or pure Spirit.

And this is why, on both a human and a spiritual level, kinship in Spirit is of superior value. Spiritual relationship is geared toward mutual advancement in God-awareness. Other relationships can also be important, but they cannot match the highest common good that is derived from communion through infinite Spirit. "Who is my mother? And who are my brethren? And he stretched out his hand toward his disciples and said, Behold my mother and my brethren! For whosoever shall do the will of my Father which is in heaven, the same is my brother, and sister, and mother" (Matthew 12:48–50).

September 26

Lahiri Baba's Mahasamadhi

Lahiri Mahasaya's Samadhi Temple,
Swami Keshabananda's Ashram, Haridwar.

Today marks the date that Lahiri Mahasaya left his body in conscious union with omnipresent Spirit. During his life, he remained a loyal and dedicated disciple of Mahavatar Babaji, initiating Hindus, Muslims, and Christians alike into Kriya Yoga, the ancient science of thought, breath, and life-energy control. Though not well known beyond devotees drawn by his irresistible spiritual magnetism, his fame grew with the publishing of the

Autobiography of a Yogi, and now millions have felt the touch of his grace through reading about his life and words of wisdom.

As devotees of the Kriya tradition, we feel a special bond with the great master. A couple of experiences come to mind in thinking more directly about how the master has blessed me. One such occasion happened to both Larry and me as we walked in scenic Lincoln Park. As we ascended up the path, we came to a magnificent deciduous tree. We had been speaking of things concerning the spiritual path when suddenly we both felt the powerful presence of Lahiri Mahasaya—we felt it at the same time as we approached this tree—the master was invisibly present under its branches. It was a powerful feeling, and to that point, I had never felt the master so near, or so powerfully. Even now, as I think back through the many years since that day, I feel the blessings from that experience.

Another time, when living on Holden Street in West Seattle, I had come home from work and was meditating in the evening. As I sat cross-legged on my meditation blanket, the master appeared before my inner vision, haloed in Light. He slowly descended from a levitation height and touched the carpet in front of me. I spontaneously bowed at his feet, and to my astonishment, I felt the flesh-and-blood touch of his feet. The master was not there in vision only, but in body. In my wonderment, I did not utter a word, but the master smiled a blessing and then the atoms of his body disbursed. Oh, what a wondrous feeling remained long after the master's body had left.

Great masters such as Lahiri Baba continue to bless us—his commitment to Kriyabans continues though he does not usually sport a body these days. We can read the stories about him and think about what it would be like to meditate with him in his parlor at his Benares home. Nevertheless, who he is in Spirit is not easily comprehended. What we may know is that he is a joyous expression of omnipresent Spirit, merged in the universal

Divine Consciousness. His blessings, which he has so graciously bestowed, have given me such a close feeling to my Lahiri Baba. My heart melts in divine love at the very thought of him. Though I can only imagine the loss the disciples felt at his passing, I know, through my own experience, that he is a living force for the upliftment of all lovers of God, and that his joy is contagious to all who are attuned to him.

September 30

THE BIRTH OF A MASTER

Lahiri Mahasaya.

On this day of September 30, we celebrate the birth of Lahiri Mahasaya—born in the village of Ghurni in 1828. The great Bengali master is the headwaters of a spiritual revolution. The master came into the world at the direction of his great guru, Babaji. Babaji was introducing the concept of the householder yogi: one who is in the world, but not of it. Like Kabir before him, Lahiri Baba demonstrated and taught that formal renunciation was not a necessity in order to attain the highest states of realization. It was the wish of Babaji and Lahiri Mahasaya to not only bring in a new lifestyle for aspirants to follow, but to give the refined pranayama meditation practice of Kriya Yoga to help accelerate the spiritual evolution of all sincere aspirants.

No individual becomes a master and perfect teacher without daily making innumerable decisions to attain that high state. After working a full day, the master would engage in nightly meditation. Like all aspirants, he experienced gradual states of unfolding that both purified and taught him along the way. Lahiri Baba focused on the Light seen at the ajna—sometimes that light became a form. It was his own Atman or Christ-self he was seeing. In this Light, he also perceived his great guru as that same Light—the inner and the outer merged and became one. Once he had a form of Light come out of his own body—all these experiences worked to release him from the bondage of ignorance and separation. Although he had already attained Nirvikalpa Samadhi on meeting his master, there were many more experiences for him to go through before attaining the ultimate liberation of Brahma Nirvana or Sahaja Samadhi.

Even as he continued to ascend his spinal stairway of realization, he taught those who came to him and saw him as their guru. For Lahiri Baba, the scriptures of India were not merely historical persons, places, and actions. In weekly Gita classes, he peerlessly taught that these were actual descriptions of what goes on in the three bodies and in the mind of a disciple when attaining realization—thus, the *Bhagavad Gita* and other historical texts were seen in the light of Kriya Yoga, and in the light of inner spiritual experiences. As an intrepid explorer and forerunner to his disciple Sri Yukteswarji, his disciple's disciple, Paramhansa Yogananda, and his disciple's disciple-disciple, Yogacharya Mother Hamilton, his wisdom penetrated through the outer layers of these ancient stories to perceive the most perfect metaphors for realization laid out in story form before all humankind. Wisdom that is seemingly hidden, but truly in plain sight. He handed down this revolutionary view of the scriptures to new generations of disciples and all of humanity—this is truly an essential part of the great master's legacy.

Lahiri Mahasaya was not interested in limiting forms of religious practice, but only taught those methods that were liberating in and of themselves and could be of maximum utilitarian use for practitioners. He was a most practical of teachers. He taught of no forms or images of God, but if disciples found inspiration in such forms, he did not make prohibitions against their use. "Striving, striving, striving, one day behold, the Goal!" was not just something he recommended to others, but was indicative of his total dedication that took him all the way to the fullest realization. Whether a sincere devotee was a postal worker, a Muslim, Christian, or of low caste, it made no difference to this universally realized master. His compassion was not limited by outer circumstances. His grace was, and is, open to all.

The great master did not profit from his role as a teacher. He took a job as a tutor after retirement to help make ends meet. Monies he took in from initiation, he passed on to Babaji. Truly, he was the noblest and most wonderful teacher and guru—a perfect example for us all. I have seen teachers surrounded by wealth, focused on by thousands, and even displaying powers and making themselves famous in the bargain. However, I would not trade any amount of time with those teachers for a moment of sitting with Lahiri Mahasaya in his little parlor in quiet meditation, being absorbed in the Infinite expanse and endless glory of his Divine Consciousness.

Simplicity, perfect joy, keen insightful wisdom, and purity of thought, word, and action are all defining virtues of this great master. I thank God and Babaji for the day Lahiri Baba was born into a human body, for the great gift that he is, for the Kriya Yoga he taught, and for the supreme wisdom he freely gave to all sincere aspirants who sought shelter at his holy feet. May we too find such shelter and be led into the highest states of realization by this supreme master, our para-param guru, Lahiri Mahasaya.

October 6

FULFILLMENT IN MARRIAGE

Rama and Sita: a true spiritual union.**

We are on our way to Victoria to join Rose and Bob in making their marriage renewal vows—after 50 years of first making their commitment. Along with raising beautiful children, working hard for many years in Prince Rupert, then moving to Victoria, they have lived a full life together. They stand as a testament to what marriage can be at a time when the idea of marriage is doubted by many. They show respect, kindness, and support at every turn. Like all relationships, it does not mean there have not been differences along the way, but they have negotiated these and matured lives well-lived with one another.

Before marriage is thrown out by new generations looking for something less committal, we should understand the virtues of—why marriage? It fulfills so many functions, on so many levels, it is not possible to note them all in a short space, or perhaps they can never be limited to a list, but let us look at a few.

Marriage was developed in ages past, not merely as a means of collecting and passing down property, or proclaiming ownership of another person; these dynamics came as a result of darker ages. Although there is an economy in a committed relationship—statistics bear out that couples who complete high school, get married before children, and stay married, do far better financially than those who do not. So, there is practical financial sense to this arrangement.

Also, children reared in a long-term, committed relationship do much better on every level. Even when couples that stay together fuss and fight, state studies that span dozens of years. So, it is definitely better for children. And there are the other practical advantages. Sexually-transmitted diseases, which are epidemic today, do not happen to those who remain true to their beloved one. Making sensible plans about having children when a couple is ready means abortion is not necessary, children can be financially prepared for, and there is time for working out who does what (as there are great advantages to working together as a team). Even with so many clear advantages to marriage on these practical levels, there are even more compelling reasons for making this commitment for life.

The psychological growth that happens when a couple work on their relationship within a marriage is unparalleled. As individuals, we evolve, and so will husbands and wives need to evolve in a marriage. We are not the same person we were at 20 as when we are at 30 or 40 (usually, that is thankfully so!). These many changes demand good faith negotiations and a baseline of mutual respect. Moreover, respect is a must for any healthy relationship. Master often spoke of overfamiliarity as a primary problem for couples, and, of course, he was exactly right. We learn that our words, tone of voice, and attitude all matter, and this is most apparent within a marriage of a husband and a wife. The demands of a changing nature combined with learning the value of respect, can merge with the ability to negotiate through differences with a basic "stick-to-it-ness," and are powerful maturational processes that help us to become wiser and more tolerant with time.

An even deeper element than the psychological maturity that comes with a healthy marriage is spiritual bonding. As we change with time and grow psychologically, there are also spiritual heights of union between two souls that become as one in God. Nature does a remarkable job of simulating spiritual union with new sex. Many times, in those initial encounters, ego boundaries collapse and there is a total joining of body and mind. It can feel perfect—in the moment. Then the differences come in, and we can spend a lifetime trying to get back to that first union, or we can go from relationship to relationship, seeking that magic.

The real magic is in going to the next level attained through psychological harmony, and then on to spiritual union. There are no quick, "Five Minutes to Spiritual Union" books. A couple who works out many of the psychological rough edges may then, by going further, come into spiritual union. This union transcends time and space as it unites two souls. While the two will hold differences on a human level, they still can experience oneness in spirit—a dropping of boundaries, and entering into a peaceful sea of Soul connection—a transcendent merging of two souls that are as one in God.

There are souls who stay together through the years, working out the rough edges with no success—only drinking from a bitter cup. Some work on their relationship with some degree of growth, and there are others who really find that level of mutual respect and mellow into a fine patina, like a well-made and cared-for artwork. Then others achieve the ultimate merging of souls, and are able to maintain that over time, a true spiritual union—this is the ultimate fulfillment of marriage, in addition to the many other great advantages. God's presence felt in such a spiritual relationship lifts the hearts and spirits of all, and God greatly blesses such ones—they are the true power-couple. May we be blessed to find such a spiritual union with another if it be His will, for us to find a soul to be with on such a great adventure.

October 10

THE LECTIN-FREE EXPERIMENT UPDATE

The new appeal of greens.**

We have continued our lectin-free diet (as outlined by Dr. Steven Gundry)[26]. Lectins are the plant's way of protecting itself from predators (and yes, we are plant predators). The actual degree that lectins make people sick may be disputed; however, it is the doctor's contention that their cumulative effect over time, along with poor eating habits by many, in combination with the frequent use of antibiotics, combine to destroy gut health. The recovery of good gut health helps eliminate autoimmune disorders and diseases.

---

26   *The Plant Paradox.*

With the health of the gut in mind, we began the program: a three-day cleanse, followed by a six-week, less-restrictive cleanse; then, we entered a third phase in which we could add one food a week, eat it a few times, and observe if there were any autoimmune reactions. If not, then we could add that food to the yes list. If there is a noticeable reaction, then it is to stay on the no list. My baseline started with already following a gluten (gluten is a lectin) and diary free-diet, something I had learned to do over the past twenty years to avoid the kind of autoimmune reactions we are talking about: painful joints, and excess mucus in the sinuses. Even though I was following a gluten/dairy-free diet, I had developed joint pain once again, as well as sinus headaches when waking up in the morning (I was starting to think my body was feeling old, especially in the a.m.!)

I had reported to you in an earlier posting the results after the first six weeks (we first started at the beginning of June). Fast forward four months, and now here are the results: joint pain is gone, sinus headaches are gone, physical energy is smoother throughout the day, and food cravings are non-existent—this is interesting. According to the good doctor, the bad bacteria in the gut (stomach, small intestine, and colon) communicate directly with the brain through the vagus nerve system. Bad bacteria want foods they like: sugar, fats, cheap carbs, etc. Eliminating the bad bacteria, eliminates their cravings! I have to say, that is born out in our experiments. Desired weight loss has also been a result. Carla lost some stubborn last few pounds she was working on for some time before. I have lost 10 percent of total body weight, and I am in clear sight of where I would like to be, weight-wise.

Note: nuts and nut butter are part of the plan, and when I hit a weight loss plateau, I eliminated nuts and nut butter, and then my weight continued to drop. In addition, not only have food cravings disappeared, but my desire for greens has gone up; the good bacteria are asking for what they like. In fact, we have liked the foods so well, not missing any of the old items—literally, not missing them at all. We have not really looked into adding foods to the basic program post six weeks. So, I have to say that the experiment has gone very well; these are all positives, and there are no negatives except for the fact that, when traveling, eating out is a challenge—Thai food is a pretty good source for staying on the plan (Mediterranean food would also present good possibilities). Also, Carla has had to put a fair amount of effort into finding and learning to prepare food items. There are some online sources that have helped, as well as exploring local sources. So, thumbs up for Dr. Gundry's lectin-free food program to this point. My body is definitely feeling younger!

Supplemental: There are dietary supplements that Dr. Gundry recommends; in a few cases, he tells you about other companies that also provide these supplements. Supplements are not mandatory for being on the program, but we have added a few. I was already taking probiotics from my oncological naturopath, but we have been using his prebiotics and his Vital Reds product. We like them both; the Vital Reds are especially satisfying. This said, Dr. Gundry has turned into a supplement machine—his ads can be a turn-off. But, as I say, there is nothing in the program that demands these products. One additional note, we have purchased his cookbook—all the recipes have been from good to really good. We have purchased an Instantpot and have enjoyed foods made by this method. As Sri Yukteswarji advised: follow any simple diet which proves suited to one's constitution.

October 13

FOIL YOUR FOIBLES

Krishna dancing on the head of the
serpent, Kaliya: Stay true to the path.**

Generally, as devotees, we know what our foibles are: anger, greed, fear, and lust are some of the big ones. Any one of these can trip us up in our sadhana; therefore, we must keep a steady vigilance against these obstacles to realizing our true Divine Nature.

Fear had not been a typical problem for me, but there came a time in my meditation when it fissured from some unknown depth—this unpredictable emergence of a contrary thought, or emotion, can happen to any devotee due to latent tendencies buried deep in the subconscious mind. When this fear came up, it made me want to be anywhere other than sitting on my meditation asana. I thought, "It would be so easy never to meditate again as this seems to be the only time this fear comes." But some better part of me knew that I must overcome this emotion in order to make spiritual progress; running away was no solution. So, I returned again and again to the battleground until I eventually worked through fear's many layers.

Sometimes the lurking opposition is not so obvious—a subtle force behind the scenes makes us shy away from going deeper. It is not until we really challenge it that the obstacle reveals its vicious tenacity and its true name. Thus, we can remain only surface-deep in our devotions, pretending everything is all right, but all the time, not making any real spiritual progress. We must work at keeping ourselves on that edge of growth—not overstraining and not slacking, yet ever looking to improve.

Sadhakas do not have anyone following them around to make sure they are doing all they can to make spiritual progress; they must be self-correcting, and challenge themselves from their own desire for Self-realization. Each person's progress is determined by his or her own self-direction. It is not a matter of just putting in time; we must make our time count. Ask, "Do I feel ever-new joy? Is there peace and an inner stillness at the core of who I am, and what I do? Is the Divine Presence with me day and night? Are my thoughts, words, and actions worthy of being a child of the Infinite?" These hallmarks are indications of true spiritual growth and they let us know when we are making progress.

We have been taught by Mother not to settle for "Mister In-between." And why would we rob ourselves of our rightful heritage? To know the joy, bliss, light, wisdom, and power of God's all-embracing Presence makes all the things of the world appear as mere baubles. We think this world is wonderful, and there is no denying it is a marvelous creation, but in comparison with the greatness of God inside of us, it is as nothing. Let us bless ourselves by taking the spiritual adventure of a lifetime; let us be *in the Know* and get the *Insider information* that boosts our God-stock—it only ever goes up, and it never loses its value! Touching the hem of God makes us drop to our knees in disbelief that this divinity has been secreted away in the recesses of our Being all this time, yet we never knew it. It is then that we stand in wonder as to why it took so long to make the effort, to go deeper, and to soar higher.

Travel Notes: *Go West, Young Man:* Carla and I plan to shift to the Southwest desert soon. I feel the pull of the desert as a place to work on writings, both Mother's and my own. Mother and Master went to the desert at important times in their work, Master going often to write, and, as a result, we have his pre-eminent Gita and New Testament commentaries. Om Sri Ram Jai Ram Jai Jai Ram!

October 16

YOUR MOTHER WAS RIGHT!

Mother Hamilton: A Teacher of
Timeless Truth, London, 1977.

Our spiritual mother, Mother Hamilton, was right. I have chosen from a list of things that make you live longer according to some of the most recent articles. I was struck by how many things have proven Mother to be right. Take a look at the list.[27]

---

27   Editor's Note: This discourse has been summarized as science and research changes over time. For the original, visit: **www.crossandlotus.com**

- Say "Om": meditating, even for just a few minutes each day, can dramatically improve your outlook, emotions, and health.

- No amount of alcohol consumption is healthy.

- Quit smoking: the single most important thing anyone can do for their health is to avoid tobacco or quit smoking.

- Get hitched: married people live longer than non-married folk.

- Look to a higher power: people who attend religious services at least once a week tend to outlive those who do not.

- Start a gratitude journal: grateful people feel healthier and report fewer aches and pains.

- Find your calling: find a calling that gives you purpose.

- Give back for the right reasons: volunteers who lend a hand for selfless reasons live longer than those who don't volunteer.

- Go Dark: chocoholics rejoice! Dark chocolate—with a minimum of 70 percent cacao—can lower stress and inflammation and improve mood, memory, and immunity.

- Stand your ground: don't back down; a stubborn disposition (strong will), may give you an important edge—a longer life.

- Order chicken instead of steak.

- Don't vape: studies shows that adolescent users get just as much nicotine with e-cigs as they do with traditional ones and they found that vaping may modify the DNA in the mouths of users, which could increase their cancer risk.

- Enjoy a cup of coffee: enjoy, unless you get headaches, an irregular heartbeat, or gastric upset from drinking coffee.

- C'mon get happy: some studies show that people who scored highest on measures of optimism had a lower risk of death from cancer, a lower risk of death from heart disease and respiratory disease, and a lower risk of dying from stroke.

While Mother did not teach us to eat chocolate or drink coffee, she did enjoy both. I know she would agree that they are not beneficial for everyone if they have negative side effects. She asked us to promise not to drink alcohol, smoke, or use recreational drugs, and asked that we have no sex without the benefit of marriage—as it turns out, Mother was right!

October 23

LIFE IS SUFFERING—AND MORE

Sacred suffering heart of our Beloved Lord.**

In his first of the Four Noble Truths, the Buddha taught that life is suffering—the Sanskrit word is Dukkha (dukə). Dukkha is a word that is thought to have originated from how an axle fits into the hole of a wheel. If the fit is good, it is called sukha and provides a smooth ride. If the axle is off-center, it is called dukkha, and makes for a bumpy ride. The Buddha taught that the nature of life in general provides a bumpy ride. There is no one English word that translates the word dukkha, but there are sutras from Buddhism (Hinduism has these same concepts pre-dating the Buddha) that describe dukkha as birth, aging, illness, death, sorrow, lamentation, pain, grief, despair, association with an unbeloved, separation from loved ones, and not getting what is wanted.

It seems that God has had it in mind that I should be sur-rounded by the swirling waters of dukkha at this time. Perhaps it is an ugly turn of the stars, but there seem to be a lot of axles in life, giving a bumpy ride to many sincere souls seeking realization. What is difficult for the sadhaka, is to know that he or she should not be attached to the ups and downs of life, yet suffering is so compelling to the mind—it glues itself to the object of suffering, as if it were the all in all.

It can be tempting to see the suffering of another and wonder why it is so upsetting to him or her or to thank one's lucky stars that it is not our situation. But compassion, the universal vision, makes all lives deeply connected with one's own; therefore, the suffering of another is not simply something to be seen from a distance, but it is a part of us. To be useful to another experienc-ing such suffering does not require that we too become identified with the object of suffering, for that would be the blind leading the blind, but for us to remain in our oneness with God while also being conscious of the suffering of another.

Conscious oneness with God aligns the axle—it smooths the bumpy ride, and keeps life moving in the right direction. It is inev-itable that when the road is filled with potholes, there will be bumps galore! However, the true axle will see us through every difficulty. I was in close connection with Mother Hamilton as she traversed some of the bumpiest roads I have ever witnessed. Strokes, heart attacks, and a severe case of shingles on her face and head that made her convulse in pain without respite—my goodness, what a tremendous load she carried! I thought of myself being in her situation and I could not see how I could go on. Yet, I watched in astonished amazement how Mother negoti-ated these treacherous roads, always telling the truth about her condition when asked, but determined that she should ever serve God and that she should recover full health.

Mother gave me an up close and personal tutorial on how to keep the axle perfectly centered, even on her road of tremen-dous suffering. And those lessons did not go to waste as God proceeded to put me through all of the experiences He had been orchestrating for me: from loss of family and home, vocation, and health, going through the "nothingness of God," the emptying out of the cup of the mind, and scouring it of everything I could call my own—until the chaff was separated from the kernel, then the seed was ground into nothingness and made fit to enter the fires of God's oven. I truly needed to have that time with Mother to show me the stuff of which I would need to be made in order to go through all that God had in mind for me.

Now I can be with the suffering of this world; it swirls around me, but I know that I am not that. I feel the sorrows, losses, pain, and misery of others deep within me, yet there is a deeper knowing of Reality that shines beyond every dark cloud—and this makes all the difference. That we may all know this supe-rior Reality, that each one's axle stays true, even through life's many bumps, is my greatest thought and prayer for each one of you. If asked, Mother would say exactly what pain and difficulties she was going through—and through it all, she was a fighter. For every difficulty, there was a solution; for every pain, there was healing in the here and now, or in the offing—she sought out God's healing directly, and God working through physicians and healers. And she was not waiting to feel better to serve God. She served God all the way through, always focused upon doing His will at all times, and in all places. Master, too, went through great suffering, as did Sister Gyanamata, Papa, Mataji, and Swamiji, all so tremendous in God—all suffered in the body, even after, perhaps especially after, achieving oneness with the Divine.

If we suffer, we are in good company. Surely, we should do all in our power to remove the thorn causing the pain. And even while in the midst of suffering, look for that which is beyond the clouds of doubt and the agony of the moment. There is a part of the mind that focuses itself on the pain, like drivers slowing down when going by a traffic accident, looking for those who are injured. Yet, there is a superior Reality that is not to be missed. When I was at Anandashram, I was greatly suffering from an illness;[28] I asked Papa to show me how pain and bliss were the same. He inwardly responded. I saw him in a vision as he took my hands, and with a toothless grin, began to dance with me around and around in blissful joy. There was a part of the mind that knew the body was still in pain, yet I felt such bliss. Bliss and pain, pain and bliss, they merged and truly became the same. Be this true for you as well when life's bumps test the trueness of your axle.

Pilgrimage update: We have spent a beautiful couple of days in Ashland with Peter and all dear friends there. Ram's wind then blew us east, across three 5,000-feet-plus mountain passes and on to Lakeview. At an altitude of 4800 feet, it is known as "the tallest town in Oregon." We are on our way to Salt Lake City, and from there, we plan to have the darshan of Nature's cathedrals in Zion and Bryce Canyons. Jai Gurus!

---

28   Editor's Note: This may have been when Yogacharya David had typhoid fever.

October 28

TALKING WITH YOUR DIVINE FRIEND

God as your friend: Child Krishna hugging Swami Satchidananda,
drawing by Gargi (Lakshmi), Anandashram.**

One of the most intimate ways to be with our Maker is to be in conversation with Him throughout our days and nights. Union with God presents a variety of ways to be in relationship with our deepest Soul connection. Since it is quite human to talk as a means to share information, and to grow closer by sharing our deepest thoughts and feelings, why would we not converse with our Heavenly Father/Divine Mother in just that way?

What a resource we have in God—a confidant, friend, and wise counselor are just some of the contacts we might have with the Infinite. The key in all of our spiritual practice is, "What makes us feel close to God?" When struggling with something in life, it is so wonderful to place it before our Divine Friend. "Lord, you have given me quite a problem. What shall we do?" Then open to listening as well as talking. I once heard a wise saying, "Prayer without meditation is like asking a question without waiting for an answer." So, you must learn to be quiet for one-God-blessed-moment to listen to what God might be thinking about the subject. The mind is so busy talking, usually repeating the same worries over and again, all the while going in circles, without stopping long enough to receive inner direction. A conversation must be two ways for it to be truly complete.

So often, when we are up against difficulties, we immediately feel alone, and feel that we are without anyone to help. Reaching out to the Supreme Beloved breaks the circle of isolation into which we have placed ourselves. One thing we observe: the more stuck we are, the more alone we feel. When we connect with God, we practice humility, for much of isolation comes from pride and shame—which are two sides of the same coin. We think, "I can do this. I will not ask for help from others—I don't want to be seen as inadequate." Then we suffer from the tremendous weight of pride, and it sinks us. Humility opens the door to Divine help, especially when we need it most (and, in truth, we need it at all times).

To feel that we have a friend in God makes our heart glow. God laughs with us, cries with us, enjoys a sunny day with us, and commiserates on rainy days. Our Divine Friend is the only one who can be with us always: from the birth of the body to its last breath, before we come into this incarnation and far beyond when we continue our adventure. God creates us, so He knows us more intimately than perhaps we know ourselves—so there is nothing to hide. Oh, what a friend we have in God! So loyal, patient, with solace in heart and mind, when you come to Him in earnestness. To cultivate this friendship makes the Infinite available to us day and night: a witness to our trials, a collaborator in our tests, and a dispenser of joy when we accomplish something worthy.

Start this collaboration with the Beloved—sincerity is all that is required. It is we who have kept the door closed, so we must open it with our honest approach to Him. Simply, we must open our heart to our Heavenly Father, receive the warm comfort of our Divine Mother, play with our beloved Friend, and talk over our troubles with our wise Counselor. Let us walk hand in hand in times of peace, so that when trials shriek, we need only reach out, and there we will find our most sacred Beloved. Even when going beyond duality's realm, He is our very Self; the "conversation" continues as He is with us as divine thoughts that move through our mind, and as sacred emotions that flow through our heart. So, whether in duality or beyond, God is the one constant that takes us through all stages of life and is ever our well-wisher. Let us deepen our conversation with Him now and we will discover that our Friend of friends is waiting for us at this very moment.

Travel Note: We are currently in Salt Lake City area and plan to leave for southern Utah to commune with the Divine Mother's natural wonders—taking our pilgrimage to Her Natural Cathedrals.

Prayer Note: Let us pray for the families, friends, and those who were at the Philadelphia Synagogue who were attacked by a man in an act of senseless violence. Let civility be the watchword for encountering those who are different from ourselves. As Master used to say, "Fools argue, wise men discuss." Let there be civility, kindness, a desire to understand another's point of view—a desire to find the common ground of universal kinship upon which to build lasting relationships with all men and women. Hate and intolerance are not a solution—only mutual respect and love heal.

November 1

THE MYTHICAL DRAGON

St. George subduing his dragon.**

God was talking to me yesterday morning—I have the most interesting conversations with Him—He was speaking of dragons. In the East, dragons are seen as powerful portents of good luck. However, in the West, dragons are pictured as greedy; they hole up in the base of mountains, jealously guarding their gold—both in the East and the West, dragons are generally thought of being snake-like with the ability to fly. These polar-opposite associations of good and bad dragons in the East and the West reflect the changing imagery of snakes from the Old to the New Testaments.

In the Old Testament, the snake is subtle, and a source of temptation: the cause of the fall of humankind, and the eviction of man and woman from the Garden of Eden. The dragon in the West is greedy, sitting alone on a pile of gold, and if anyone challenges its riches, it defends the pile of gold with angry fire. Symbolically, this snake-dragon of the West represents the lower forces in humankind, such as greed, lust, and wrath. The dragon does nothing productive with this gold but only miserly sits on it. Its fire is an aggressively destructive response to greed. There is nothing good, nothing redeeming, about this dragon.

St. George subdues his dragon; he does not kill it but is pictured with his spear projecting up above its mouth. This has an important meaning. St. George has mastered the lower forces of lust, greed, and anger; the spear represents the spine, with the lower energies channeled upward to the higher centers. In the New Testament, Jesus refers to the serpent as wise and says that it must be lifted up, even as Moses did in the wilderness (John 3:14)—St. George has accomplished this difficult task.

A dragon from the East on the Cloud Mountain Retreat Center mantle.

In the East, the dragon is in the positive, elevated state, with the power to give boons to the deserving supplicant. The dragon's ability to fly means it has uplifting power, and it also has mastery over water, which symbolizes consciousness. We see the dragon in festive array during New Year celebrations, being paraded down the street with the idea of bringing good luck for the new year.

However, once we understand the symbolic meaning of the dragon, we know it is not a mythical being to pray to or petition for good things; rather, it represents an active power inside of us that can act for good or for ill, depending upon how we direct our thoughts and life-energy. With pure intention, we focus on lifting this powerful force up the spine—raising us into realms divine. What an opportunity we have in this lifetime to not simply grovel deep in the base of the mountain, sitting in the dark, full of greed, lust, and anger. We can take wing and fly amongst angelic stars of heavenly consciousness in the bliss of our heavenly kingdom.

I bow to the Divine Mind that has taught me about these universal symbols—unfolding their meaning so that we might all learn to soar.

Travel Note: We are currently encamped near Moab, next to the Colorado River. There are over a hundred feet of a sheer wall of red stone rising out of the other side of the river. The days are sunny, the nights cool. We will explore Arches National Park, Canyonlands, and nearby, are the Red Rock canyons where most of the John Wayne movies were filmed, along with Indiana Jones, and many other movies. Three years ago, we were here when it was discovered that I was bleeding internally, so anemic the doctor wondered how I managed to walk in the door of the emergency room—rather than be carried in! It was the beginning of quite a medical journey. It is interesting to note, I have only positive associations with Moab, the medical past seems to be a lifetime ago now. Perhaps the dragon found me worthy and has blessed me. Surely, we are blessed by the Infinite, both within, and without.

November 4

MANY LIVES IN ONE

Delicate Arch at Arches National Park, Utah.

It seems that within any one life, we live many lifetimes, seemingly not only distinct chapters in a life, but entirely separate books. Abrupt changes, intense situations, and altered consciousness can make for radical chapters, book endings, or beginnings in an unfolding life. Returning to Canyonlands near Moab has brought about just such a recognition for me.

It was just three years ago that Rick, Judy, Carla, and I were strolling amongst vast canyons here with their fantastically shaped rocks—one stone looks like an immense whale, another is called "Cleopatra's Chair" (she would have had to be hundreds of feet tall to fit in that chair), immense stone buttes called the Merrimac and the Monitor from Civil War fame, and wide-cut canyons from the Colorado and Green Rivers, backed by snow-clad mountains. Even if you are not generally a fan of rock and stone, you cannot help but be impressed with views such as the one from Dead Horse Canyon. Three years ago, unbeknownst to me at the time, I was extremely anemic and as I walked a very slight grade of a paved walk to view the Green River far below, I found myself stopping every few steps to catch my breath—it finally dawned upon me that I should make a visit to the emergency room; the body was in trouble.

What seems another lifetime ago now, I went through various medical procedures that removed what turned out to be stage four melanoma cancer from my internal organs—part of my small intestines, and a few months later, some of my liver and all of my gallbladder were excised (I think they were having a two-for-one special that day at the University Hospital). If there were any more incisions made on my stomach area, I could play a neat game of tic-tac-toe on the eight and eleven-inch scars left behind. Come forward a little over two-and-a-half years since the last operation, now being cancer-free, Carla and I walk up a three-mile path that is called "difficult" on the guide map to Delicate Arch. I sprang up the rocky ascent like a gazelle (well, okay, at least in my mind I felt like a gazelle). Feeling full of life-energy, it was a fun challenge for us to get to the top and then look down upon this amazing exhibit of nature's art, viewing from a sixty-foot-high stone arch, surveying a deep valley below. There is a lifetime of difference between the first pilgrimage here three years ago and today.

The concept of time is a strange one. Circumstances can make a desperate moment seem like forever, and in happier situations, time speeds up. In some chapters and books, life can go by almost without us knowing that time is making us flow downstream, gobbling up years, and other times are condensed—all compact, and densely-lived. Whether the plasticity of time appears slow or fast, we have but one absolute measurement that is our polestar in life to help us keep our bearings and make us know who and what we are—to be consciously aware of our true Self.

It is knowing our true Self that grounds us to timeless truth, freeing us from being simply swept up in the time-current of the moment. The seas of our life can be stormy and wind-tossed, with crashing waves all around us, or it can be open blue skies, placid, and silky smooth. Whether we are in our ups or our downs, there is a singular spiritual Presence that is ever the same—calm, pure, steady, and always a comfort and a guide. Time and experience teach us the superior value of being in communion with this Presence as it proves itself to be our one, true, reliable friend and guide throughout all time.

Whether it be one life or the many lives we live, there is but one great lesson to learn: to be in a state of Self-realization that slips past the grasp of time and space and weds us to the Eternal. There is something here in these ancient towers of stone, a multibillion-year-old earth that speaks to the listening soul. It tells of ages gone and ages yet to come. It vibrates a deep sympathy to a quiet soul. It teaches us to measure time in a completely different manner than humans normally do, and it hints at a quiet understanding that all is well. How quickly a human life must seem to these ancient sentinels, how fleeting our concerns and worries. These ancient ones teach us patience and perspective. They demonstrate that great beauty rises from their midst, and then they crumble back into source once again—in all these comings and goings that span hundreds of thousands of years, these stalwart ones whisper, "All is well, all is well."

Travel Note: We are encamped on the Colorado River in a valley—so our internet comes and goes, and even at the best times of day, it is not strong. So, we will not be broadcasting today, but hope to do so soon—we will be with you in Spirit. Next, we plan to have the darshan of Monument Valley, which is located on the Utah-Arizona border on Navaho land. It will be our first time in the Four Corners area, so we are looking forward to the next adventures Ram has on the itinerary. One thing is certain, Moab and its surrounding area are a favorite for both of us.

Colorado River near Moab.

November 8

AMAZING MONUMENT VALLEY

A glimpse of Monument Valley, Utah.

Amazing may very well be one of those overused words that gets thrown into too many conversations—or, on the other hand, everything in this creation is truly amazing because it is all made up of God-stuff, and therefore it is extraordinary from its very inception to its eventual end. We have just been to Monument Valley on the Navaho's land in southern Utah and northern Arizona. If anything deserves this special designation of amazing—it is here.

The floor of this extensive valley is made up of the most beautiful brown soil, with blue and green low-growing shrubs stretching out as far as the eye can see. Like stalagmites, enormous Buttes jut up from the floor, giving rise to nature's monuments—and in the process, they create natural cathedrals of great proportions. Why red rock is so much more pleasing than gray is a question I am not sure how to answer; however, this rock makes these extraordinary landscape-shaped works of art sculpted by the Divine Mother's hands of wind and rain.

We drive upon the valley floor on a rough road as guests of the Navaho Nation. We are sympathetic to their notion that this land is sacred. We hike on a trail circumambulating a large butte and pass under polished cliffsides of amber, red, and black—we are in simple awe of this projecting mass high above us. Then, our gaze turns horizontal and looks out to the monuments scattered across the valley that, in the far distance, forms a continuous fortress wall. We note not only the visual beauty but also the feeling of purity and expanse. Every now and then we exhale deep sighs in acknowledgment of profound relaxation, our spirits' response to what is clearly God's country.

The Three Sisters.

How do I describe the feeling-nature of this place? It is elusive, deep, and healing—actually, in the end, it turns out it is indescribable. In an earlier posting, I spoke of the rock and stone speaking to my soul; more than a poetic muse, it is an underlying reality, both then and now. For the earth speaks to us when we are quiet and listen; rocks, trees, and all of nature vibrate with their own consciousness—and as with all creations of our one Creator, each part has the Divine Essence at its core. Equally, just as every human being has individual differences, so does every part of creation exhibit its own personality. In Monument Valley, there is a special purity that speaks to the soul, a healing force of nature.

Walking amongst these enormous monoliths, there is a feeling-vibration of the eternal Spirit; relative to a human's life, these monuments are ageless, solid, and unmoving. Although we know that ancient nature cannot truly embody eternity as Spirit does (for it comes and goes as does all creation), nevertheless, these rock formations communicate a timelessness through their very core-essence. We feel blessed to partake of their spirit and are reminded of Jesus' response when he was told to quiet those around him who were joyously singing God's name, "If these should hold their peace, the stones would immediately cry out" (Luke 19:40). Does the Master not proclaim that stones also sing the name of God—perhaps even more readily than sophisticated humankind?

I glimpse into the purpose of the divine plan for why He has brought me here. Stone and rock, tree and shrub, bird and walking-creeping-crawling creatures all reveal that God is all in all, and that He wishes me to see and participate in the amazing mystery of all that He has created. Time and again, He proves that not only is universal Spirit omnipotent, omnipresent, and omniscient, but He also delights in the unique signatures He inscribes on every particle of space.

Today, we have continued our journey-pilgrimage to Flagstaff, Arizona. At 7,000 feet elevation, we are surrounded by pine forests, and on this black night, overhead, shines a brilliant Milky Way. A photon emits from some distant star or galaxy and travels millions, perhaps hundreds of millions, of years at 186,000 miles per second only to end its long, long journey in the retina of my eye—it registers in my brain as a distant point of light. Through the interaction of light and eye, that distant star and I are joined. Oh, what a magnificent, amazing universe we participate in. God so delights in revealing His mystery in every life, every situation, and in every soul. May He awaken the amazing in you so that you may feel your connection and oneness with all that He is.

Travel Note: At Monument Valley, we stayed at Goulding's R.V. Park and Resort. The Gouldings have an interesting history—a love story: a testament to the tenacity and to the surprising results that can happen when people are determined.

West Mitten Butte, Monument Valley.

November 11

ALL IN HIS LOVING HANDS

Vulture Peak, Arizona, a favorite spot.

t is inevitable that while living in a human body, there will be pain and suffering, no matter how perfectly one lives. Swami Satchidanandaji told me that when Joel Goldsmith was at Anandashram, Swamiji had the opportunity to drive Joel to the train station. Swamiji took that opportunity to ask Joel a question that was on his mind: "When you were speaking here at the Ashram, you did not touch on a theme you write about in your books; that is, if you think positive thoughts, you will have perfect health. Why not?" Joel said that he did not speak on that subject when he was in India because people would inevitably ask him if that were true. They would ask, "What about Ramana Maharshi?" Ramana Maharshi had the highest realization and also had many physical problems—such as walking completely bent over, due to severe rheumatoid arthritis. Swamiji summed up Joel's answer, saying, "Unproven theories."

There is no doubt that thinking in a positive manner, following good health principles, and eating the right foods will increase our chances of avoiding physical problems, but the fact is that the body is subject to ailments and various problems that occur in life, some of which come from past karma and must be paid for. While we should do all that we know to lead a healthy life-style and avoid doing harm to ourselves and others, nevertheless, there will be times when pain and problems find their way to our doorstep. It is then we are faced with how we will deal with such problems.

There are some things we should definitely not do. A common association is made when problems come—we entertain the idea that things always go wrong; a pity party of one ensues and makes a *pig-pile* of troubles that link difficulties from the past, and pro-jected problems from the future, to making it seem intolerable to bear what is occurring in the present. The first thing to do is to disconnect remembrances from the past and from anticipated horrors about the future, and simply stay focused on the here and now. Once it is narrowed down to the present, acknowledge that God is supplying everything we need to endure, and even rise above, the current situation. We may have to go through what God is giving us, but we can affirm that it is God who is doing the giving and realize that His grace is with us.

There is a secret that saints have known through the ages, and that is shared passion. The passion of the Christ is all Jesus went through during the crucifixion (Passion: from Late Latin: *passio-nem*, meaning suffering, enduring). As the story comes down to us, the crucifixion happened over three days. It is a story that condenses the different stages of the crucifixion in a way that is similar to the description of how God made all of creation in six days. Each day is a stage or segment of creation—for how could there be anything that we call a day before the sun and earth came into being? Creation came in six stages, and the three days of the crucifixion are also three stages—one representing the physical, another the astral or energetic, and the third, the idea or causal body. We too go through these stages, but one day, one year, ten years, or more, may be required for each stage to be complete.

So, to get through these stages, saints think, "I am sharing this feeling of being crucified with the Christ," or, "I am on the battlefield with Arjuna and Krishna," or, "I am in the night of testing with the Buddha." By putting the mind on a divine personality going through these experiences, there is a link made between the human and the divine that allows grace to enter into the experience. This grace brings strength, even joy, during anguish and removes the fear and the isolation that so often come with suffering.

Jesus did not ask for pain; in fact, he asked, "If possible, let this cup pass from me" (Matthew 26:39). Arjuna asked Krishna if he could leave the field of battle; Mother Hamilton said she was no fool, and did not ask for suffering; but in all cases, they all fulfilled divine will by staying the course as God directed them. This leads to another important idea: what we go through is not without meaning—there is a purpose behind everything we are put through—that is especially true when we create a pure intention to seek God alone.

When we know there is meaning behind all our experiences, then we can endure so much more. When we feel that God and Guru have forgotten us, and they do not see our pain or suffering, then we can go down a spiral of despair. When God gives us a tremendous load, the bridge supporting that great weight may creak and groan, but this only indicates the stress of what is being transported, not a lack of faith, as this is exactly what God has asked us to do. In our deepest soul, we feel that this is what has been given to us; it is His will, and we are privileged to be sharing the load that He must carry on a daily basis. For God is all that is; therefore, He is suffering with all the pain that all of creation experiences—He feels everything that every person goes through; He knows the reason for which everything occurs, and He knows that it is fulfilling a high purpose.

Papa assures us that for everything that goes wrong, we are brought closer to surrender. It is only when we come to that point of complete surrender that we enter into total union with the Infinite. So, suffering brings us to realization, and realization is the cure for suffering. It is not that Papa did not have problems physically, financially, and socially, but he surrendered everything that he was, and he knew that all happened by the will of God, and therefore, even suffering was God, and in that, he realized that pain and bliss were the same and that knowing brought the end of real suffering—that is separation from God.

Every day, God gives me a load to carry. If I did not do all that I have written here, it would be impossible for me to carry out His will. He has not abandoned any one of us; therefore, He is with us, each step of the way. Let us feel His grace, even now, picking us up and helping us to put one foot in front of the other. That even when the bridge carrying the heavy weight moans and groans, His grace is supporting us in doing His will; His strength is ours; His grace is flowing in our veins and sinews, and His wisdom is directing us. All is in His loving hands.

Travel Note: We have had the darshan of the Grand Canyon with its magnificent views; however, it did not have the same depth of feeling that was present in the previous sites recently seen.

Currently, we have once again come to Vulture Peak—it has been three years since we were last here. It has always been a favorite spot for us on BLM (Bureau of Land Management) land.

All blessings to you on your journey and may you ever know that you are in His loving hands.

New Moon on the rise opposite Vulture Peak.

November 16

O DEATH: WHERE IS THY STING?

Grand Canyon, Arizona: Even the millennial plans of
nature as revealed in the Grand Canyon are simply
blips of time in comparison to the eternal Soul.

Anyone who has seen a corpse, I think, must be struck not just by the absence of the signs of life, such as breathing and movement, but something subtler—it is the lack of life-energy, and an indefinable finality. There is Newton's maxim for the conservation of energy. He speaks of the fact that energy cannot be gained or lost, but it simply changes form. So, the body's elements return to their source, *from dust to dust*, a few dollars' worth of chemicals. But what of the life-force for one such as Newton, his ambition, intelligence, and feeling-nature? Do we define this as the soul? If these traits are products of biochemical reactions, then they die with the chemistry set of the body. However, if consciousness is more than the body, and the soul is more than electrical stimulations to neurons, and if art and poetry are anything other than an aberration, and if the pursuit of mathematics and science are more than accidents of nature without design, then we must admit there is also more to religion than a philosophy driven by the fear of death, or the desire to control others through issuing an "opiate to the masses."

Any thinking, sensitive, soul knows that within the sensate being is something beyond adaptations to surviving a hostile environment. Religious expression through art, literature, and song, lifts the soul above grubby nature and offer a sublimity of experience that can make one soar as on the wings of angels. There is a driving force in life to challenge the physical limits of consciousness. What happens to this drive when the body is no more?

If someone wedded to the body says, "I only know this body, this world. If there is more, why do I not know it?" You might as well ask the mud worm what lies beyond its murky world, for it takes its own incomprehension of anything more as proof there is nothing more to the world than watery or dry soil. Or, if you ask the fish about the sky, the fish might shudder with fear, thinking that the sky is death, and responds by swimming into the depths at the mere thought of the airy vastness. And ask someone whose world is his or her patch of earth about celebrating life by rising in a hot air balloon to see the curvature of the earth—and going further, all the way to the edge, where the blue sky turns black and reveals vast galaxies beyond—and the person simply looks at you as if you are mad. Each one, the mud worm, fish, or earthbound human, is conditioned by perceptual-imprisoned thinking that what is beyond is something to be feared.

However, the spiritual-adventurer chafes at artificially-imposed limits. Just as a racehorse gets his blood up looking at the racecourse, so does an aspirant for higher truth yearn to run the course. The aspirant strains to burst the bounds of the sense-shackles. Oh, to defy the gravity that glues feet to earth, to rise above mundane matters and soar upon those angels' wings! To go further than even what the poet paints in words, the artist seeks to invoke on canvas, to even go beyond the heights that song can inspire! And where does this energy, this power of mind, heart, and spirit, transcend when death claims its share? Soul cannot be created or destroyed, but only change form.

To **know** what soul without body is does not require a final death. This is the secret of religion. Krishna, Buddha, Jesus, and Mohammed were explorers of what worm, fish, and human know not. They claimed this truth, not just for themselves, but that we all shall have the capacity to go beyond, to go where no human has gone. Humans cannot know this ultimate Truth, because he or she is no longer human when they realize they are more than body, more than mud, more than water. The power of the quest transforms humans into an overarching Soul, free of the limits of body, name, sex, or vocation; he or she is changed into something new. That power does not simply disappear—just the opposite—it becomes immortalized.

For the realized aspirant, the eternality of Soul is just as plain a fact as it is for the astronaut when the sky turns from blue to black and the earth transforms from flatness into being round—Self-realization reveals the Soul as it has always been, will always be. The tiny limits of human perspective, which seemed all-powerful before, are now broken forever. Life is not only eternal, but beautiful beyond compare; it is no longer filled with sorrow and despair, but joyously blissful. Life is not dark and obscure, but enlightened, full of inspiration, meaning, and wisdom. What has always been will always be—and that "always" part is the essence of not only the individual Soul but the essence of all that is. It is as if life before was a dark dream, a life lived in a cavern of shadows, and it has now awakened to a world of light and color.

In that realization, we may joyously sing with St. Paul, "O death, where is thy sting? O grave, where is thy victory?" (1 Corinthians 15:55). For we now know the greater Reality in which nothing is lost: though the body may return its *dust to dust*, the Soul returns to its eternal life in God.

November 18

LIFE'S PORTRAIT: DECISIONS, ACTIONS, AND REVELATIONS

Sower with Setting Sun, painting by Vincent Van Gogh, 1889.

I t has been very interesting reviewing Mother's talks as we have been going through her transcripts from the 1980s. In thinking back over Mother's life, there are definite hallmarks that stand out: taking incarnation on Christmas Day in 1904; meeting Master in 1925; Mother being made minister, and then Yogacharya in 1948 and 1951; Master leaving the body in 1952; Mother attaining Nirvikalpa Samadhi, and meeting Papa and going to Anandashram in 1954 and in 1957; returning to India in 1967; attaining Sahaja

Samadhi in 1970; going to India again in 1978; then traveling to the South Sea Islands, Australia, and New Zealand in 1981; entering into what I have called a second Mystical Crucifixion; and then there was her Mahasamadhi at the beginning of 1991. These broad-brush strokes of Mother's life give a wide-angle view of a life lived in service to God and Guru.

One may also look at significant moments in Mother's life, the fine-brush strokes in her life-portrait. Such as when she came to Service one Sunday and said that God had revealed to her the famous "missing link" in Darwin's evolution idea—the missing link being there is no evidence for an evolutionary transition between lower species and humans. Mother said that God showed her this link from animal to human occurs in the astral realm, and it cannot be explained by simple genetic jumps. Or, when Mother stood up—as Elisabeth Haich had said to Mother—and proclaimed, "I am that I am!" And the wonderful experience Mother had in doing this significant action that freed her once and for all from thinking she was insignificant. Then there was the moment when Mother confirmed with the fully-realized master, Swami Ramdas, the revelation that God had given her—the scriptures are, in reality, the story of everyone's evolution from the human to the divine. As Swami Satchidananda commented, it was a moment of great truth!

Every life may be seen from its broad strokes all the way down to its micro-moments of decisions, actions, and revelations. Mother's life took many unexpected turns, for both herself and those around her. God's will can seem inscrutable at the time, and it may take the perspective of generations to appreciate what is being accomplished. Jesus' life looked like a disaster at its end. Jesus was horribly killed, and his disciples fled in every direction. To the Sadducees and Romans, it was only a tiny blip at the time, and then for hundreds of years, small groups of followers met in secret. All but one of the twelve disciples were killed for their beliefs. Jesus' life and death did not look like much at the time, much less did it have the appearance of being a world-changing event.

And those micro-moment decisions, how they can affect so many! Master returned to India in 1935. He considered not coming back to America. He wrote to Rajasi that he was "in a fix," if it was not for Rajasi, and a few others, Master would not return. And how we have all benefited from the fact that God prompted Master to continue his work here! And when Papa left hearth and home to follow God's will by becoming a sannyasin, and when Mataji left her home to be with Papa, amidst storms of criticism—so many decisions are made in the moment upon which the world turns—and we are thus benefited.

I remember being at the Van Gogh Museum in Amsterdam. A guide explained how his pictures are made up of so many tiny dots. When you stand close to the painting, you see many, many fine-colored points that do not really make sense. Then, as you take steps away from the picture, those dots begin to coalesce into flowers, rivers, trees, and reflections in water—it all comes together into a beautiful portrait. Who could have known this when seeing only tiny strokes of color up close? In this way, we may see our lives as so many little actions and decisions throughout the day. Those little decisions may seem insignificant on their own but without those tiny dots of action, there would be no larger picture when we step back to see what has been created.

God has taken me on many adventures in this life; some of which have been inexplicable at the time, even contrary to what I thought should have happened. Yet, from the perspective of a few steps removed, those decisions, actions, and revelations create pictures that illumine His plan. Even those things I thought were mistakes at the time, they all add up to something beautiful for God. When mistakes equal learning, and learning produces growth, then even what does harm in the moment can be made to serve a higher good in the end—those crazy dots not only make the picture interesting, but the darkish shadows make the brightness all the more brilliant.

God has, in recent years, certainly led me on a journey that is different from what I would have thought beforehand. He took me on a proposed circumambulation of North America, only to have it interrupted by illness. Then, after the delay, onward around the continent, not so much to see people, although this too is part of the journey, but majorly to see natures and human-made cathedrals. Now, He has us traveling to the Southwest's desert, seemingly away from you. He does not have me seek out people-connections but seems intent upon Nature's Cathedrals, and most of all, to be inwardly communing with Him.

Now, this inward communion can and does take place any-where and everywhere; so why does He bring me here? It is a mystery. Outwardly, I can sit down to read a book, but I spend an hour lifted up in Him and barely read a page! He draws me unto Himself. I merge into His Being, and through Him, I merge with all of you. Those are the dots, and through the dots, He is painting His masterpiece.

Oh, Ram, Oh Lord, You alone know the ins and outs of Your plan; You alone can know what You are creating and why. I know that You only do good. So, in being in You, Your will brings about the highest good for all. Meanwhile, each dot, each moment, is lived in You, and is keeping Your will—that is what I know.

November 22

GRATITUDE ON THIS THANKSGIVING DAY

Yogacharya David, Snake-Columbia River Confluence, Washington, 2016**

O n this holiday (holy day) of Thanksgiving, we are brought to mind to give thanks for all those things God gives to us: our health, prosperity, and all good things. It is interesting to read in the life of Jesus, when the great Galilean Master is about to raise his dear friend Lazarus from the dead:

> Then they took away the stone from the place where the
> dead was laid. And Jesus lifted up his eyes, and said, Father,
> I thank thee that thou hast heard me. And I knew that

thou hearest me always: but because of the people which stand by, I said it, that they may believe that thou hast sent me (John 11:41–42).

Jesus thanked God before the fact because he intuitively knew what God was going to do. There is a great principle being demonstrated in his thanksgiving, which puts the individual into right relationship with his Creator. It is one thing to give thanks for what has been given, but to give thanks for that which is to come opens the floodgates for grace to flow to you.

When you have challenges of health, prosperity, and relationships, inwardly commune with your infinite Beloved and give thanks, knowing He knows all that you need, and His great love and desire for your good to come to you is even now doing so. Giving thanks is an affirmation of what is even now coming to you in multifarious ways.

When he approaches the tomb of Lazarus, the description of the Master is the shortest sentence in the entire Bible, "Jesus wept" (John 11:35). Jesus felt his grief, the grief of those around him, and tears poured from him. He inwardly petitioned his heavenly Father, "Can nothing be done?" And then he knew that God was to do something tremendous. A man lying dead for four days, and God would work a miracle. Jesus knew God had heard his heart's cry and he wanted others to know that what was to happen is coming from God, not himself. So, he spoke out his thanksgiving to his Heavenly Father for what was to come.

When in need of healing, God may heal you directly through grace, He may also send to you the right people or circumstances to enact healing, or He may give you strength and perspective to endure what must be gone through. And this is true for prosperity and broken relationships as well. It is also the way in which you achieve God-realization—God, even now, sends you all you need in the present, and for what is to come.

When giving thanks, you feel a loving relationship with God. It is grace that is coming into your body: giving it all that is needed for healing, providing material prosperity as it flows to you in unknown and delightful ways, healing relationships in you and in others—it all comes from the exhaustless storehouse of He who creates vast universes. While His Presence is beyond the scope of the puny little human mind to encompass, He also comes in personal, loving, and tender ways to each person, and to all parts of His creation.

Thank you, Lord, for giving me the awareness of Your Presence, for in that deep connection with You, I have everything that You are. I live in the prime simplicity of Your Being—I am merged in You, and You in me. And through Your all-powerful Presence, You may fulfill Your will for me, and for this world. I give You thanks, not because You require it, but because it puts me in right relationship with You, because it helps open the inner floodgates of Your power, intelligence, and love. You create all that is and all that is to come, and for what You give, I offer You my most humble and loving gratitude.

Happy Thanksgiving Day to you, and may every moment of every day be filled with gratitude for the greatest gift of all—the living Presence of our Infinite Beloved.

November 25

LESSONS FROM THE SPORTS FIELD

Mother Hamilton, our supreme Guru-Coach, 1978.

When I was in Junior High and High School, I was an avid sports player and fan. From a young age, I had player-cards from my favorite New York Yankees baseball team that came from buying bubble gum (I didn't care about the flat square gum, only the cards that had pictures and stats on the players): Mickey Mantle, Roger Maris, Yogi Berra, and more, all adorned the inside of my bedroom door. And football—my team was the Green Bay Packers with Bart Starr, Jim Taylor, and Ray Nitschke. Then, for years, I was not interested in sports—and now, I enjoy a good football game on television.

Whether you care for sports or not, there are lessons we can draw from those who play—as we can see from anyone who practices an art, skill, trade, or craft at a high level. Even in the top echelon of players, and in the best teams, there are always fumbles, dropped passes, and missed tackles. There is no such thing, even amongst legends of the game, as those who make every play. The lesson we can learn and apply to our spiritual efforts—is that we, as do they, aim for perfection, but we understand that, spiritually, we will drop passes of inner direction coming from God; we can fail to tackle and contain ignorance, and we can fumble away our spiritual connection with God.

Watching the players coming to the sidelines after making one of these mistakes, we see them communicate with their coach. My football coach would occasionally grab my facemask (that would be called a foul if done on the field!) and talk in a forceful voice, inches away, to make sure he had my full attention and that my mind was not wandering when he was giving me his wisdom (Mother could do the same in her own way!). Coaches, are foremost—good teachers. They encourage full effort, excellent concentration, and making good choices, in split seconds. So, there is a learning moment with the coach on the sidelines, when he encourages you to shake off a bad play and get focused on the next. All good lessons for being on the spiritual playing field.

Sports demand individual effort, but they are also team endeavors. There is a balance in these concepts, and one understands that the individual player is responsible for fully participating, and that he or she is also part of a team effort in which victory comes from everyone making their best and brightest contribution, and that the coach is essential for directing the strategy and teaching tactics of the game.

As aspirants, we too must take responsibility for making our best effort, to recognize the value and synergy of being on a team of devotees, "For where two or three are gathered in my name, there I am in the midst of them" (Matthew 18:20). And, the guru-coach helps us to make superlative individual and collective effort, ever directing us toward being victorious—that we might all become one with God and help lift this world into higher consciousness.

Yogacharya David from his Gridiron (high school football) days, a picture from the Sunnyside Sun Newspaper.

December 2

OH, WHAT A MYSTERIOUS LIFE

Sunrise in Borrego Springs Desert, California.

It is a mysterious life God has given me. Mysterious in the sense of being inscrutable, unpredictable, full of power and glory that is beyond description, and dependent upon a Divine Will that puts some things in the scrap heap and then suddenly propels other things forward without hesitation.

Mother tells a wonderful story of the time there was a disciple of Papa's who wanted to go with him when God directed Ramdas to go somewhere. The disciple had heard and read Papa's accounts of his travels and was probably thinking they would go on some marvelous adventure. Well, one day Papa said that Ram was directing Ramdas to walk across a field—so the disciple joined Papa in high anticipation. When Papa got halfway across the field, he simply turned around and started to walk back to the ashram. The stunned disciple asked what they were doing.

Why had they turned around? Papa said that Ram had suddenly directed him to turn around, so he did. Such was Papa's total surrender to God.

And, I find it to be so in my life. As I look back, it has been a life of discipleship now for many years. Decades of powerful forces that Mother unleashed in this form, many years of His power and glory intermingling their influence in my life—governing and shepherding, and gradually transforming the body, mind, and soul into a living manifestation of His Light.

It has been years of testing, as oppositional forces of desire nature, fear, and obstinance fought for the control of this form. Though I made uncountable mistakes, somehow God and Guru never let go of me, though I let go of them. Due to this grace, I learned, changed, and became something new, yet it is a state of consciousness that is deeply familiar—as if it has always been true, always been me. My old life is now seen as something long ago—it is as if I have lived many lives in this one lifespan, some of them almost unrecognizable as being me.

Yesterday God kept me wrapped in His power. I barely moved more than a few feet all through the day. Incredible forces move through this form, of such magnitude that, if they had come in this strength years ago, they would have completely overwhelmed this system. There is no doubt that it is the Divine One controlling it all. A few times, I needed to remind Him that the elephant in the hut need only move a little and the whole hut will collapse! As it is, the hut shudders from these inner fountains of light and glory.

He lets me do one thing and not another. It reminds me of the saying from Exodus that speaks of focusing the mind on things other than the Divine Presence, "Thou shalt not bow down thyself to them, nor serve them: for I the Lord thy God am a jealous God" (Exodus 20:5). Of course, this does not mean that God is jealous, as in a human kind of jealousy; rather, it is a matter of inner attunement.

The world may want one thing from you, but God is going in a different direction. On a human level, you may think that you should be doing one thing, like going across the field and beyond, but God wants you to do another, like turning around after going half-way. To be fully attuned to God, you must be willing to go against this world, even go against what you humanly think are your obligations.

There was a Methodist minister/missionary who was staying at Anandashram when Mother was there. He was inspired by Papa and very intensely wanted his God-realization.

As Mother said:

> One evening—I must tell you an interesting story about this—he decided that he would go to an old temple ruin up on top of Snake Hill. And he was going to stay there and meditate until he got God-realization, because he had been filled with bliss as he sat at the feet of the Swami. And so, he went without telling anyone but me. Night came and they couldn't find him anyplace. Papa started worrying about him and he sent some of the boys out to see if they could find him. And they searched every-where, and they couldn't find him, and Papa became quite concerned. And he said to me, "Do you know where he is?" I said, "Yes, I do, Papa, but he asked me not to tell." And he said, "Is he at the ruin at the top of the hill?" And I said, "Well, it could be." Finally, he sent the boys up there, but Paul didn't want to come down; he was going to stay. And they went back two or three times; finally, he condescended to come down. And he said, "I only came because Papa, being my guru, sent for me." And Papa made the statement, "Sometimes the Guru tells you something outwardly to test you, but inside, he is hoping that you will make the other decision."

What Mother calls "Snake Hill" is probably Manjapati, the hill behind Anandashram. There were many nights when I made my way up that hill to meditate under the full moon. I was warned a few times not to do so, due to the fact there were venomous snakes living on the hill. One day, at the ashram, a small snake was discovered that caused a lot of excitement; it was only about six inches long. It was one of the most venomous snakes in the world! I saw how easy it would be to stumble across one of these going up the hill, especially in the dark. Even though I was told not to venture up the hill in the dark, I felt it was Papa directing me to climb up with the moon as my torch. If it was his will that I should die in doing so, then so be it (what better way to go than following God's will?).

And surely, this is true for all life—to be in His all-powerful grip, acting according to His will, is to live as God truly meant His disciples to live. So, there are emails I have read but not responded to; there are projects needing attention but left to languish in the moment; there are friends and loved ones (that, if I were responding to my own human desires) I would make sure I called or wrote to, but that task, too, goes unattended. I leave it all in His hands, I have the freedom to be imprisoned in His will, and there is nothing I would rather do, nowhere else I would rather be.

In this moment, I am looking out on desert hills and a desert expanse. It is here that He wants me to be, and it is here that I am to fulfill His will. I am steeped in His Presence, His power, His glory, His bliss, and the Light of His Being. Oh, what a mysterious life He has given me.

December 9

YOU HAVE A SEAT AT THE TABLE

The Annunciation, painted by
Edward Fellowes-Pyrnne, c. 1899.

When it comes to your search for God, it can be one thing to say that you surrender to Him, and quite another to truly let it all go and lay everything at His feet. It is common to hear someone complain to God, "I don't like this, and I don't like that!" But complaining is not surrender; rather, it is often the very essence of attachment—an ongoing negotiation with God about what is not right with the world and how it should be different.

In a seeming contrast to surrender, Sri Yukteswarji, then through Master and Mother, very clearly knew that the most powerful way to invoke the creative power of God was not to go to him as a beggar, "Oh Lord, I am a most miserable sinner, and while I do not deserve this, will you give me_____." Rather, the master thought only of going to God as a rightful heir, each claiming his or her lawful inheritance, "Lord, I am made in Your likeness and image. I now claim my natural state of abundance, perfect health, and total realization."

What do these two approaches have in common? In both, total surrender, and through prayer-demand, you know that you are not outside the window looking into the banquet of God; rather, you are at the table of the Infinite as one of the sacred family. In both, God is not some distant personality to whom you beg a few crumbs or stand back from in abject misery of separation—instead, right attitude heals the breach: you merge your little self with God's great Self.

This is the measurement by which you may know that you have perfectly surrendered, or that you have attained the right state of mind in prayer-demand: you feel deeply connected with the omnipresent, omniscient, and omnipotent Spirit in and around you. You may work to achieve these states by practicing surrender and affirming prayer-demands, but there is a qualitative shift that occurs when you quit being on the outside and you place yourself as a full member at God's table.

There was the night Mother Mary was visited by an angel that told her she would bear a child, a holy child. There must have been so many thoughts that came into her mind. First, how was such a thing possible since she had never been with a man? Then, there were very real consequences: the shame of being pregnant and not being married, that dire law, she could be shunned by her family, rejected by her fiancé, and even stoned to death! With all this hanging over her head, she surrendered to God's will, "And Mary said, Behold the handmaid of the Lord; be it unto me according to thy word. And the angel departed from her" (Luke 1:38).

Such perfect surrender gives peace, inner assurance, and strength. It does not mean that everything is going to go perfectly smoothly. As it is told, the birth of Jesus is filled with horror as soldiers are sent to kill the infant. The little family had to flee to the distant country of Egypt to save their lives. However, inner direction led them to safety; it also took them home when the time was right and it sustained them with strength and the needed abundance throughout it all.

Whether claiming your right as a lawful recipient of all that is God's, or being in complete surrender to His will, let your heart be at peace; feel the Divine Presence full to overflowing within and without. The life of Jesus is replete with examples of manifesting God's will for healing and abundance, and also accepting what is, in total surrender to the Supreme One's will—each according to its own season. May this sacred time of celebrating the birth of Christ Consciousness into the world, and into the human frame, strengthen your resolve to be in seamless union with the ever-perfect Light of your Heavenly Father and Divine Mother.

December 20

SPREAD YOUR WINGS

Mother Hamilton's picture on Yogacharya
David and Carla's home mantle at Christmas.

Christmas traditions do make it "A Most Wonderful Time of the Year," as the song proclaims. For our Northern Hemisphere, and as we climb in latitude, the prolonged dark days make decorative light displays inside and outside of the house bring additional meaning and beauty. Seasonal music, foods, the exchange of cards, greetings, and get-togethers, all make for a festive spirit. Of course, most of the wide world does not celebrate Christmas but what is universally known are the subtle, powerful currents that occur with the seasonal solstice.

For millennia, yogis and mystics from every nook and clime of the world have recognized the subtle, but powerful, effects of different times of the day, the year, and the movements of the zodiacal clock. I have never made a study of astrology, but I have had experiences with some of these dynamics. On a few occasions, I consulted an astrologer who Mother had also gone to see. One such time was when I injured my back at work, and it became clear over the months that I could no longer perform the hard physical labor of my current job. I had inwardly felt prompted to pursue a degree in psychology, but I was concerned because it would initially mean going back for a university degree, and, at least for a while, making less money than I had been—I was concurrently responsible for providing for a family. With that in mind, I went to see this astrologer with an open mind but some skepticism. I had only provided my birth information to her when I sat down for a "reading."

She proceeded to tell me that I had recently injured my back (there was nothing obvious in my physical movements that would have told her that), and that if I continued in my current work I would be crippled, due to a lack of fluid moving in the spine. Later, I asked my doctor about this, and he said that could be a very likely result. She also said that I should be a teacher or a counselor, and that, at first, the money would be less, but eventually, it would be all right—all of which turned out to be true. She touched on many other aspects of my life, but this was the salient point for that visit. It proved to me that there was something to astrology; her accuracy and specificity were remarkable. She did get the time off a bit when she said, "You recently hurt your back, six months ago." It had been only three months before, not six.

Other experiences with solar and lunar influences have included an awareness of the full moon effect. I have an increase in energy during full moon cycles. This, by the way, is always a positive influence, waking me up earlier in the morning and keeping me up later at night to meditate—the energy provides a spiritual uplift. And when the earth makes its way around the sun and we approach Winter Solstice, I am aware of powerful forces at work.

For many years, this had stirred up difficult psychological thoughts and moods. At some point—some years ago now—those difficult moods left, and now I only experience these forces as uplifting currents. A third area I have been aware of is the sense that, when either events proceed with extraordinary smoothness, like all the skids are greased, or it is like fighting uphill all the way, and it is as if the stars have taken on a helpful or a difficult turn. There are those times when what was difficult suddenly changes, like a magnet flipping its polar ends, and what was repelling before is now easy. There may be other explanations for this experience, but I have a sense that the stars certainly seem to figure into these shifting winds.

One of the principles that yogis discovered is that you can take full advantage of these recurring cycles. For instance, with the Winter Solstice, you can deepen your meditation, and spread your wings, so to speak, to take advantage of these uplifting currents. And while these active solstice forces may stir up difficult psycho-emotional energies as well, they can then make this is a time for purification, as it is your spiritual work to pass these subconscious moods into the Light. It is valuable to be aware of these invisible, but powerful, forces and use them to your advantage.

So, even as you are enjoying the hustle-and-bustle demands of the season, and there are many lovely traditions to take advantage of, as a householder-yogi, you should also be cognizant of these subtly-powerful currents as you approach the Winter Solstice. Take time to read sacred texts and meditate deeply. Take inspiration from these magnificent words from a wonderful God-man, Isaiah, from nearly 3,000 years ago:

> To whom then will ye liken me, or shall I be equal? saith the Holy One. Lift up your eyes on high, and behold who hath created these things . . . Hast thou not known? hast thou not heard, that the everlasting God, the Lord, the

Creator of the ends of the earth, fainteth not, neither is weary? there is no searching of his understanding. He giveth power to the faint; and to them that have no might he increaseth strength. Even the youths shall faint and be weary, and the young men shall utterly fall: But they that wait upon the Lord shall renew their strength; they shall mount up with wings as eagles; they shall run, and not be weary; and they shall walk, and not faint (Isaiah 40:25–31).

December 23

BLISSFUL MUSIC

Song of the Angels, painting by
William Adolphe Bouguereau, 1881.

There are many mediums that have been used to lift up consciousness: art, architecture, and poetry, but none is more powerful than music. Last night, we gathered and sang Christmas songs. What a lovely feeling there continues to be from the power of song focused on the sacredness of life.

Once God gave me a vision in which I saw the angels gathered about God's throne as song filled the air. I had never really been attracted by descriptions of this sort of thing before; I did not understand the appeal of sitting on a cloud, strumming a harp. Mother once quoted Master, saying that this idea did not appeal to him, either. He said, "My God, how boring!" And that is how I felt about it. However, in this vision, how do I describe it? The angelic music was definitely music, but also variations of bliss. And those angelic souls were like meditating yogis, enraptured with the ever-new bliss that also manifested as music. It was unusual and absolutely magnificent. How I wish everyone could sit on the throne and experience the power, the unbelievable beauty, and the always-fresh and pure feeling of this blissful music.

Songs to God here on earth are expressions of this same principle. There are so many truly lovely Christmas songs. It makes it special to keep those songs only for this time of year. And, like those angels about God's throne, songs to God can be holy and filled with varying vibrations of infinite bliss. This is what I continue to feel this morning.

Bliss is a most interesting phenomenon. It is always identifiable as bliss. A common signature is that you know it when you experience it. Yet, within that unity, it is constantly changing—ever-new. All the world looks for what is new out there, throwing away things of the past and focusing on the latest and greatest. Yet, residing right in our own beings is this tremendous source of power, light, and ever-enthralling bliss. The name of God in India is Sat-Chid-Ananda, and the last, Ananda, means Bliss. It is one of the eternal verities of the Infinite.

This world is full of divisions. However, underlying all divisions there beats the unifying rhythm of bliss that ties everything together in perfect harmony. Certainly, this world is here for us to enjoy, and part of that enjoyment is the variety of variegated expressions. To bring all of these multifaceted creations under one roof requires a universal principle, and that is the presence of God, weaving a musical theme of bliss throughout all creation. So, during this season when we sing out the promise, "Glory to God in the highest, and on Earth, peace, and good will toward men" (Luke 2:14), let us find the bliss within that makes this promise a reality—even now, even now.

December 24

A Christmas Eve Meditation

Adoration of the Shepherds, painting by Gerard van Honthorst, c. 1622.**

S tories are such wonderful teachers. The story that has grown up around the birth of Jesus—an avatar coming to bring salvation to this world—is captivating, and it makes one feel intimate with that holy family.

We think of a star-studded night; the shepherds are having an extraordinary vision of angels, a promise fulfilled from ancient times: a night of wonder and glory (Luke 2:8). So inspired are they that the flocks are left, and a search is made for the fulfillment of the angels' prediction—to find a babe wrapped in swaddling clothes, lying in a manger. What a charming sight it brings to mind, to think of shepherds in rough woolens and simply-shod, coming in reverence and awe due to the angels' appearance and what was said. We know those blessed shepherds are uplifted by this experience because we are told they return to their fields, glorifying and praising God.

We then jump from Luke's account to Matthew's (Matthew 2:11), for each has their part to tell. Imagine three wise men (astrologers, reading the stars) approaching a "young child," (a young child—perhaps not a newborn—but let us stay with how tradition comes down to us today), and on that fateful night, they open their treasures of gold, frankincense, and myrrh. These gifts are of such great value that history has thought of these men as kings.

So, the scene is set for our deepened meditation. We see the angels imparting their prophetic message with spiritual power to humble shepherds in their fields, and we too experience the glory of this night, the ecstatic beauty of it all. We follow the shepherds as they proceed to a humble cowshed and shyly approach, in wonder, this newborn and his parents—we bow with the shepherds at the feet of this holy baby who has come to fulfill ancient prophecies.

Then, on their heels, we see ourselves enter in with the wise men, bringing all that is treasured in life; in blissful submission, we surrender our lives and all that we are at Divinity's feet. There is magic in the air, strange and marvelous things are afoot. We merge into the story through our deepened meditation. Divinity is born. Sacredness is awakened in us. What greater promise can be fulfilled?

Oh, what peace, what joy, and what bliss is ours! How our souls thrill at the prospect of being in such holy company. What better task than to let our minds dwell on this holy night in deepened meditation? May peace ring out from the inner depths of our humble soul, and may the promise of a divine child be born in us, bringing to life all of its fulfillment—for each person and for all of humankind.

December 25

MOTHER'S ADVENT

Mother Hamilton at Christmas, 1970s.

W e would have to travel back one hundred and four-
teen years to Christmas day in Duluth, Minnesota. I
am sure it was cold, below freezing on this special
holy day. The mother, a beautiful woman, fully expectant, but
there must have been anxiety as this was the only successful deliv-
ery, with six others who died at birth. Her father, half Iroquois,
would have looked on with silent reserve. The young family did
not have much money, so the circumstances would have been
very modest. At that time, the birth may have been at home, as
many were then.

Mother was born around noon that day; as she said, she ruined
her mother's Christmas dinner. Her life was to be terribly difficult

but also filled with overcoming and tremendous achievement. She had the love and grace of two fully realized masters in her life, and the love and recognition of many, many, saints of high realization. She lived a full life: a professional woman, a mother of three, with grandchildren, and great-grandchildren (who called her G.G., great-grandmother), and most importantly, she was a tremendous God-woman—a teacher and guide, and a guru for many.

When she walked into the room, you felt the power of God in her. She also had a lively interest in everyone she met. She always sought to bring out the best in everyone and to give them fully of God's love. With practical wisdom and intuitive insight, she guided many on the path of realization. She sowed seeds of the highest quality for spiritual growth and realization. Some seeds landed on stony indifference, some entered good ground, but too shallow, some found rich earth, but the storms of life eventually eroded the base, and those trees did not bear the fullest fruit, and then a very few cultivated the seed that was freely given into producing the most perfect fruit in God's Garden.

Today, we honor Mother. Her birth into this world was a challenge from the start, but she made the most of what she was given, and as a result, we have untold opportunities as part of the rich inheritance she bequeathed us. As she said, "If I, just this one small woman, can do it, so can you!" Mother unleashed the greatest potential in a human being and attained the highest realization of God—Sahaja Samadhi.

On this Christmas Day, we celebrate the advent of two Christ-souls: Jesus, and Mother. Both came for the sake of humanity. Both came to awaken the sleeping God within us. Both left footsteps for us to follow so that we too may exclaim:

I feel the wonder and the beauty of Thy glorious Presence in every part of my being. My heart is bursting with my love for Thee. My mind and my intelligence are radiant with Thy healing Light. I and my Father are One, blessed Spirit, I am He!

Be it so. Merry Christmas to all, and Happy Birthday, Jesus and Mother!

December 31

GOD CREATES

Hands in space with a galaxy forming between them.**

We celebrate the end of a year and the beginning of a new one. We can use this as an opportunity to take stock of what is working in our lives and what is not. There is a simple psychological maxim: "When you find something that works for you, do more of that!" And, obviously, its opposite: "When something doesn't work, do less of it!" Reflection and analysis are essential to creating better models of what works and this is a good time for doing both.

It is also a time for celebrating what has worked—what we have done well. Many of us do not take time to feel good about what we have accomplished, and so often we focus on our mistakes.

This gives too much weight to the negative. While reflection is good, it should be done with the idea of learning from experience. Obsessing about the negative only gives wrongheaded patterns of power. Let us learn from our experiences, make amends where possible, and move on in a positive way. Do not make a fetish of focusing on wrong actions; let us learn to feel good about what we have done well and then do more of that!

Looking forward to the future, do not project a bad year onto the new one. We have a blank canvas upon which to paint, an empty book with fresh pages to write upon. Sri Yukteswarji said that God creates this universe; he did not say God created, but God *creates*. We are co-creating our life with God. We are in a constant state of becoming, and each moment holds the potential for all eternity in it.

Sense this potential moment—God is in us, and we are in God. With that awareness, a vast field of potential comes alive in us, so let us not sell ourselves short. Feel that God is coming alive in us and that we do not know all that we can be. So, each day is a discovery: What does God want from us? It is an exciting time to be alive, no matter our circumstances because we are truly made in the likeness and image of God.

A very Happy New Year!

Health Update: On Friday, I had an examination by my dermatologist and on Saturday, I had a CT scan and an MRI (no PET scan is scheduled from here on out, and I have been extended to six-month checkups from the previous four-month exams). Today, I received my results online from My Chart. All scans were normal, showing no problems. This December marks three years since I was first diagnosed and had a small intestine resection. April will mark three years since the liver resection, and since that time, there have been only clear scans and my health has been excellent. The dermatologist did burn off a suspicious something on the skin and sent it in for a biopsy, which he said did not concern him. So, good news for a great new year!

Conclusion

PRAYER FOR WORLD ENLIGHTENMENT

O Infinite Light of God

You are the indwelling presence

Within all creation

Both animate and inanimate.

We pray to You

For the eradication of

All conflicts and fights

Both within and without.

We charge You with the responsibility of

Leading all Humankind,

Both individually and collectively,

To live in harmony with their highest Light.

O Beloved indwelling Presence

You see to it

That dharma—right action

Is established on earth.

And that through right behavior

Corresponding to natural and Spiritual Law

Peace will reign supreme

And all Humankind will be uplifted

To your highest Light.[29]

Om Peace Bliss Amen

OM TAT SAT AUM

Mount Temple, painting by Dennis Brown.

---

29   *Climbing the Sacred Mountain* (p. 211).

References

Goldberg, Philip. (2018). *The Life of Yogananda*. San Francisco, CA.: Hay House.

Gundry, Steven. (2018). *The Plant Paradox Cookbook*. New York: Harper Wave.

Gundry, Steven. (2018). *Summary of Dr. Gundry's Diet Evolution*. New York: Harper Wave.

Gundry, Steven. (2017). *The Plant Paradox*. New York: Harper Wave.

Hamilton, Yogacharya Mildred. (2018). *My Beloved Papa, Swami Ramdas*. Camano Island, WA.: The Cross and The Lotus Publishing.

Hickenbottom, Yogacharya David. (2023). *Discourses Volume One: 2013–14: Living a Spiritually Rich Life*. Camano Island, WA.: The Cross and The Lotus Publishing.

Hickenbottom, Yogacharya David. (2022). *Silence: Entering the Cosmic Sea of Consciousness*. Camano Island, WA.: The Cross and The Lotus Publishing.

Hickenbottom, Yogacharya David. (2021). *Climbing the Sacred Mountain: Poems and Prayers of a Western Yogi*. Camano Island, WA.: The Cross and The Lotus Publishing.

Hickenbottom, Yogacharya David. (2019). *My Spiritual India*. Camano Island, WA.: The Cross and The Lotus Publishing.

Paramhansa Yogananda. (1995). *God Talks with Arjuna: Bhagavad Gita*. Los Angeles, CA.: Self-Realization Fellowship.

Paramhansa Yogananda. (1946). *Autobiography of a Yogi*. New York: The Philosophical Library.

Sri Aurobindo. (1995). *Essays on the Gita*. Twin Lakes, WI.: Lotus Light Publishing.

Steiner, Rudolf. (2009). *The Incarnation of Ahriman*. Forest Row, RH.: Rudolf Steiner Press.

Film References

Jesus of Nazareth. (1972). Directed by Franco Zeffireli. ITC Entertainment, RAI.

Brother Sun, Sister Moon. (1972). Directed by Franco Zeffireli. Paramount Pictures.

Bible References

King James Bible Online: https//www.kingjamesbibleonline.org

Website References

Mother Hamilton's quote reference: The Cross and The Lotus: www.crossandlotus.com

Yogacharya David's original discourse reference: www.crossandlotus.com

Anandashram reference: www.anandashram.org

Yogananda, *My India* poem. https://aumamen.com/topic/my-india-a-poem-by-paramahansa-yogananda

Yogananda, *My India* poem. www.ananda.org

Thomas Paine. https://www.ushistory.org

Billy Graham information. https://www.savannahnow.com/story/opinion/columns/2018/02/24/cal-thomas-billy-graham-i/13608487007/

Image Attribution

2018

With the exception of those listed below, all images are used courtesy of the David and Carla Hickenbottom portfolio. Photos were taken by David and Carla Hickenbottom or gifted with permission by friends, family, and devotees. Attribution for images from these sources has not been included here. Images of devotees or written submissions from devotees are all included after receiving consent for this book series. Images are either paid for or for free use under public domain, Creative Commons licensing, or from other sources as noted.

January 4. *Woman's Hand with Spiritual Mystic Light* by Joseph Klopacka on Dreamstime.com. License purchased.

January 7. *San Damiano Crucifix*, c. 12th Century. Commons. wikimedia.org. Public domain.

January 14. *PY-SY*: Sri Yukteswar with Paramhansa Yogananda, Sri Yukteswar's Serampore Hermitage, India, 1935. Commons. wikimedia.org. Public domain.

January 18. *Christ in Gethsemane* by Carl Bloch, 1873. Commons. wikimedia.org. Public domain.

January 20. Swami Vivekananda at Jaipur, c. 1885–1895, shared by Ramakrishna Mission, is licensed under Creative Commons CC-BY-SA 3.0 and GNU Free Documentation License. Also in public domain. Commons.wikimedia.org

January 24. *World Religions* by Casejustin on Dreamstime.com. License purchased.

February 14. *Cross and Ash* by Czarnybez on Dreamstime.com. License purchased.

February 14. *Red Heart* by Kyzysztof Jaracz from Pixabay.com. Free use under the Pixabay license.

February 22. *George Washington* portrait by Rembrandt Peale, c. 1846. Artvee.com. Public domain.

February 22. Paramhansa Yogananda holding flowers, Mt. Vernon, Virginia, 1927. Paramhansayogananda.com. Public domain.

February 25. *Jesus and Peter on the Water* by Gustave Brion, 1863. Commons.wikimedia.org. Public domain.

March 7. Paramhansa Yogananda, 1952. Picture commonly known as "The Last Smile" by Arthur Say. Commons.wikimedia.org. Public domain.

March 18. *Road on the Sky* by Ievgenii Tryfonov on Dreamstime. com. License purchased.

March 25. *Siva Gives Pashupatastra to Arjun* by Mahavir Prasad Mishra. Mahabharata: Tej Kumar Book Depot. Commons. wikimedia.org. Public domain.

March 30. *Figure of Christ* by Heinrich Hofmann, 1884. Commons. wikimedia.org. Public domain.

April 1. *Empty Tomb* by Rachata Sinthopachakul on Shutterstock. com. License purchased.

April 4. *Christ in Gethsemane* by Heinrich Hofmann, 1886. Commons.wikimedia.org. Public domain.

April 8. *Earth and Sunbeam in Galaxy* by Blackzheep on Dreamstime.com. License purchased.

April 13. Paramhansa Yogananda and Rajasi Janakananda, 1938. Paramhansayogananda.com. Public domain.

April 15. Swami Ramdas, Anandashram, India, c. 1930s. Anandashram.org

April 29. Swami Ramdas, Anandashram, India. Anandashram.org

May 5. Rajasi Janakananda: *Rajarsi Lotus-A*. Courtesy of Ananda Church of Self-Realization. Commons.wikimedia.org. Public domain.

May 12. *Paramhansa Yogananda,* Santa Rosa, California, 1920s. Commons.Wikimedia.org. Public domain.

June 3. *Beetles Pollinate Orange Daylilies* by Olgavolodina on Dreamstime.com. License purchased.

June 10. *Thomas Paine*, portrait by Auguste Millere, c. 1876. Commons.wikimedia.org. Public domain.

June 17. *God The Father* by Giovanni Battista Cima de Conegliano, c. 1510–1517. Commons.wikimedia.org. Public domain.

June 21. *Paramhansa Yogananda and Sri Yukteswar at Solstice Celebration*, 1935. *Autobiography of a Yogi*, p. 36. Public domain.

June 24. *Sri Yukteswar*, c. 1913. Commons.wikimedia.org. Public domain.

July 8. *Lion & Lamb Painting*, painting by Clint Cearley on Shutterstock.com. License purchased.

July 12. *White Sleeping Peace Buddha Face* by Korn Vitthanyanukarun on Dreamstime.com. License purchased.

July 13. *Baby Thief Krishna* Bazaar art c. 1950s. Commons.wikimedia.org. Public domain.

July 15. *Lord Ganesha* by Pradeep Kumar Sharma is licensed under Creative Commons CC-BY-SA 4.0. Commons.wikimedia.org

July 29. *Full Moon* by Rangizzz on Dreamstime.com. License purchased.

August 5. *Sailboats at Sunset* by Richard Carey on Dreamstime.com. License purchased.

August 12. *Two Hands Preserve a Green Tree Against Thunder* by Sergey Galushko on Dreamstime.com. License purchased.

August 26. *Diagram of the Chakras* by Lahiri Mahasaya c. 1880s. Acquired by Paramhansa Yogananda in 1935. Public domain.

September 16. *Four Season Tree* by Lilkar on Dreamstime.com. License purchased.

September 20. *Rama Returns to Ayodhya*. Illustration by Balasaheb Pandit Pant Pratindhi, in *Chitra Ramayana*, c. 1916. Commons.wikimedia.org. Public domain.

September 30. Lahiri Mahasaya. *Autobiography of a Yogi*, p. 317. Wikimedia Commons. Public domain.

October 6. *Rama and Sita as a Couple*. Bazaar art, 1950s. Commons.wikimedia.org. Public domain.

October 10. *Homage to Leafy Greens* by Anne Stephenson on Dreamstime.com. License purchased.

October 13. *Krishna Dancing on the Head of Kaliya*. India bazaar art print, unknown author, c. 1950s. Commons.wikimedia.org. Public domain.

October 23. *Divine Mercy of Jesus Sacred Heart* by Prasad KB on Dreamstime.com. License purchased.

November 1. *Saint George and the Dragon*, late 15th century icon painting from Candia. Commons.wikimedia.org. Public domain.

November 18. *The Sower* by Vincent Van Gogh, 1889. Commons.wikimedia.org. Public domain.

December 9. *The Annunciation* or *Ecce Ancilla Domini* by Edward Arthur Fellowes Prynne, c. 1899, on Alamy.com. License purchased.

December 23. *Song of the Angels* by William-Adolphe Bouguereau, 1881. Commons.wikimedia.org. Public domain.

December 24. *Adoration of the Shepherds* by Gerard van Honthorst, c. 1622. Commons.wikimedia.org. Public domain.

December 31. *Hands of God are Creating Galaxy in Universe* by vchal on Shutterstock.com. License purchased.

Conclusion: *Mount Temple*, Alberta, Canada. Painting by Dennis Brown. Permission Granted.

Acknowledgments

Yogacharya David has a unique ability to share spiritual teachings and soul-enhancing reflections in a most accessible manner—he can reach us in our day-to-day ways of being as we strive to live a purposeful life. He guides us, and even as he laughs at himself, he still seriously advocates for a wake-up process.

It is a privilege to form what we call Team-David, a dedicated team of aspirants who willingly devote time and expertise to ensuring that Yogacharya David's legacy of teachings reaches those who long for a deeper, broader, disciplined-yet-freeing approach to life's journey.

Carla Hickenbottom, David's wife and senior disciple, has been a major support throughout the preparation and publication process. Her loving oversight and her diligence as director of The Cross and The Lotus Publishing support us each step of the way.

Rebecca Harvey has been a major ongoing link to data collection and historical document searches. She seems to know just where to find more information on most everything we need. Her keen eye also provides an astute read that catches the forever-escaping grammatical challenges. Mira Lutz, our other Team-David member for the Discourses, has an excellent knowledge of grammar. It is a gift of Grace to have such a fine team working to prepare and publish Yogacharya David's series of six Discourse volumes.

Our team also includes my editor, Zia Cole, for all of the Discourse volumes—our gratitude to her for her astute eye and professional expertise.

Jan Westendorp of Kato Design and Photo brings her artistic and professional book-design expertise forward when working on our manuscripts. She provides us with elegant page layouts and image refinement support, and in so many other ways, she has helped us create a beautiful series of six volumes.

Team-David feels that Yogacharya David would be delighted to know that his unique writings and teachings are available in book form for all who seek a deeper, sacred understanding of the human condition.

About the Author

Yogacharya David Hickenbottom (1954–2019) met his guru Yogacharya Mother Hamilton, a disciple of Paramhansa Yogananda, when he was a youth of 20. Yogacharya David became a Reverend in 1984, and Mother Hamilton bestowed the Yogacharya title to David in 1989.

The great Kriya Yoga lineage of India that came through Jesus, Babaji, Lahiri Mahasaya, and Sri Yukteswar to Yogananda, and then to Mother Hamilton, provides pathways to: an appreciation of, and a faith in, the everyday sacred, an understanding of higher dimensional wisdom, an integral intuitive knowing of spiritual truths, and the vibratory realms that permeate all that is, was, and will be.

Yogacharya David says: "An inner pain brought me to the path most unwillingly, and this inner pain kept me on the path. I put my shoulder to the wheel." He faced the crux of the spiritual dilemma—how to shift from the ego-driven lower or smaller human nature to a larger and luminous existence, intuitively attuned to our deeper and broader—vast—spiritual nature, thereby discovering the Living Truth. With this intense striving for Truth and Bliss, and with his Guru's Grace, David was carried through many years of Mystical Crucifixion spiritual experiences. His year in silence (2000–2001) established an inner state of stillness that never left him—and finally led him to his full Self-realization.

Also by Yogacharya David

2013–2019 Discourse Series:

- *Discourses—Volume One: 2013–14: Living a Spiritually Rich Life*

- *Discourses—Volume Two: 2015: Re-Union of Soul and Spirit*

- *Discourses—Volume Three: 2016: A True New Birth*

- *Discourses—Volume Four: 2017: Gateway to the Infinite*

- *Discourses—Volume Five: 2018: Standing on the Threshold of Eternity*

- *Discourses—Volume Six: 2019: Writing in the Book of Life*

Hickenbottom, Yogacharya David. (2022). *Touching the Supreme Spirit*. Infinite Calendar. Camano Island, WA.: The Cross and The Lotus Publishing.

Hickenbottom, Yogacharya David. (2022). *Silence: Entering the Cosmic Sea of Consciousness*. Camano Island, WA.: The Cross and The Lotus Publishing.

Hickenbottom, Yogacharya David. (2022). *Notes to Sadhakas*. Camano Island, WA.: The Cross and The Lotus Publishing.

Hickenbottom, Yogacharya David. (2021). *Climbing the Sacred Mountain: Poems and Prayers of a Western Yogi*. Camano Island, WA.: The Cross and The Lotus Publishing.

Hickenbottom, Yogacharya David. (2019). *My Spiritual India*. Camano Island, WA.: The Cross and The Lotus Publishing.

www.ingramcontent.com/pod-product-compliance
Lightning Source LLC
Chambersburg PA
CBHW051003140626
46546CB00016B/127